GOD'S MESSAGE
ABOUT 2012

To Dex
from
Chris Lee

God's Message About 2012

An Alien Saved My Life to Share This Truth

by

Charlton Lee

This book is revised from an earlier work by the author, titled, "What Science Doesn't Know and What Religion Has Tried to Hide."

This book is a work of non-fiction. All of the accounts are true and accurate. However, the names of the characters have been changed with respect for privacy. Any similarities with regard to names, locations, and incidences are purely coincidental.

ISBN: 978-0-578-09349-9

CONTENTS

"We live during a period in which mankind's preoccupation with materialism has reached its peak. The new transformation will be internal, and within this darkness lies the most powerful and beautiful treasure to be found. Equal to the intrepidity of great men who have mastered the physical realm, the embrace of our greater conscious nature must be met with full resolute and passion."

– Hhere/Ccerdi

INTRODUCTION

BEFORE I begin, allow me to make a factual statement: it was *I who made initial contact – not they to me*! Though unintentional, I didn't know my efforts leading to this event would change my life forever. A looming event was rising and much bigger than me. This change was so drastic, yet powerful, it set me on a collision course to which I could not avoid. You see, this collision was between my private life and the financial wrecking ball that was swinging heavily my way. When it smashed into my life, an extremely guarded secret about me was exposed. I have an uncanny ability to connect with anything, anyone and any level of consciousness – past, present, and future. From King to pauper, even celebrity to layman- no one thing or person is out of reach.

The period of 2008-2010 presented a series of unexplainable phenomena that cannot be accurately described through words. Also, during this period, I befriended an extraterrestrial being and for reasons far beyond my understanding, this contact began to enable the unraveling of secrets to me that was not known by any other man or woman on this planet. In return for receiving this information, I was instructed to expose the world to the truth about God, the creation of man, the alien species that has lived amongst us since the beginning of time, and the transformative event during 2012.

The recession of 2008 was a terrible time for our nation, and especially for me; this served to be the toughest period of my life. After losing my job and suffering a series of setbacks, I found myself in a place in life that I'd never thought possible. Struggling at every effort to survive, I became homeless and emotionally stripped of any hope to get my life back together. Despite my world having collapsed around me, I was desperate not to lose what little ambition or optimism that remained in me. Therefore, I kept an open mind and an eye for the slightest breeze of opportunity that blew my way. So, when I made contact with this alien and she learned that my life had been damaged and offered to help me, I quickly accepted her offer. I remember the words of my mother, "the Lord works in mysterious ways." Is this what she meant? Could it be that God is working mysteriously through this alien to save me? I wasn't sure; however, I wasn't sure about anything in my life at that time, so all I could do was give myself a chance and trust that this was the right path.

I approach this story with both feet on the ground; yet, what you'll read will sound like something straight out of a sci-fi film. After the initial contact was made, it took me almost a year to work up the nerve to take the second step. I had serious concerns that I may have opened Pandora's Box, because I started seeing bizarre faces, shapes, and things creeping around my house that almost made me piss my pants. There will be no talk of heroism or bravado; as a matter of fact, during most of my contact, I was always poised at the ready to run at any moment! Yet, knowing what I know now, I'm glad I did take the second step. This second step was a meeting with God, and it was during this meeting that I received several fascinating and joyous truths about the origin of mankind and secrets about the universe. However, the single-most joyous event that will soon take place for all humanity is the one truth more significant than the looming event of 2013. It is this great truth that I cannot wait to share with the world.

Therefore, I present this book and message exactly how it was written in my personal journal. Each chapter will unfold to reveal much of yourself in the words you'll read. In addition, each chapter progresses from one God secret to the next shocking truth about the universe and our lives. A new birth is beginning!

CHAPTER 1

THE DEDUCTION

MY determined quest to unravel the mystery of who I am dates back to the summer of 1982. I was 17, and a desire was boiling deep within me to go forth and find myself. Yet, what that task entailed was not clear, and it was buried deeply. I couldn't explain it then, but somehow I knew that the development of my psyche, behavior, and life path was intricately tied to my parents' lives. Furthermore, I understood that every family's generations are linked with complex emotional energies that are passed down from ancestor to progeny. Although a human body returns to the earth through death, these emotional and behavioral energies continue on through the next man or woman, who in turn tries to determine who or what it is. But, to what end?

Whenever I reflected about my life and my relationship with my parents, unexplainably, I'd visualize the complex energies they've passed down to me. I eventually gave this energy a name: the glob of energy. This glob has no mass or definition and would often sit in the back of my mind. It was like it was trying to make sense of itself. Concerned if I was the only teen experiencing this strange sensation, I started to pay attention to everyone around me and, strangely, saw clearly that everyone held this glob.

Defined, this glob is the reduced energy from life's matter of unresolved questions, idiosyncrasies, demons, sexual issues, and other senseless dramatics created out of fear and hatred. No one is immune to this glob of energy. Even families who are rooted in strong tradition, education, and wealth have this complex glob inside them. A glob of unanswered issues translates to confusion for a young person and even an adult, if he or she has no support system that can teach them and help them develop healthily. Especially from the start of childhood, if a boy or girl isn't nurtured with love and correct guidance, he or she just becomes a bundle of missteps and pain; the glob of energy perpetuates into something larger. Unless such an individual has some extraordinary talent in life that offers itself to a career or focus, his or her life's nuances grow into larger confusion. Obviously, there are great success stories of a person rising from obscurity to become something grander, despite the enormity of his or her struggle. I wanted to be one of those people who broke the chains that enslaved me. But, offering a greater barrier than that of answering the question of how I was going to address this glob of energy, the question arose thus: from what approach? How do I begin to address ill thoughts and correct the behavioral instability that I've inherited from my parents, who learned it from their parents and other centers of influence? These were the personal dilemmas I faced with no solutions to begin from.

During that spring of '82, I worked late nights at a local restaurant. On my route home was a late-night theater, and all movies cost 99 cents. One Friday night, the featured movie was *Pink Floyd The Wall*. The movie seemed to speak to me; I saw a lot of myself in a character in the film, Pink. I understood his growing agitation of missing his father who left home for war and was killed in action. Seeing the main movie character go through personal dramas that ranged from an overbearing mother, troubled relationships, drug use, and social prejudice, I felt his plight. Somehow, I understood the story of personal isolation and chaos- though I never lost my father to war, but suicide. With each scene, I discovered more to which I could relate. It felt as though the writer was foretelling for my future – I too will have to tear apart my own bricks that will be cemented in loneliness and indecision.

I saw this movie every night for the five nights it was shown and studied it frame by frame. Analyzing, I began to wonder if the writer of the film himself was unraveling his own glob of energy, passed on and prolonged by his parents. It was this movie that began to set the conscientious act of breaking down my own glob. I was intent to drain every particle of water and strip every particle from the bricks that weighed on me.

March 15, 1993. I remember this day clearly, because it was the day that I was discharged from the military, a career path that meant nothing to me and represented a waste of my time. I don't know what I had expected it to be like, but when I joined in 1986, no one had prepared me for a world composed of derelicts, degenerates, drunks, druggies, and just plain dumb asses. To make matters worse, these individuals were my so-called leaders. I made a solemn promise to myself that I would never follow them or pay homage to them, and this included officers! All of them were charlatans, hiding behind their rank and trying to act tough, but they didn't fool me. Like I said, I don't know what I was thinking when I joined, and to make matters worse, when I married a nice woman, trying to do the right thing in life, I ended up re-enlisting. When I think of that particular decision, it makes me want to curl up and vomit. This period of my life was neither enlightening nor progressive, and for a guy that has made a commitment to understand who he is, the military only added more bricks of prejudice and hatred to the wall of my personality. Now that I look back, I realize that I would have rather joined some missionary project and done some real humanitarian work instead of marching around and taking orders from punks hiding behind friendly uniforms, which I *never* trusted.

Heading east on Highway 70 East from Kansas to my hometown, Indianapolis, Ind., on that evening of March 15, I stopped at a remote and abandoned gas station. Thanking God that I was free from the military, I opened the trunk of my car and, removing two duffel bags of clothes and memorabilia, I threw everything in the dumpster, including my dog tags. I wanted nothing to do with that previous life, and it felt good to barrel down the highway doing 80 mph, with Aerosmith filling the air with their guitar riffs, telling me it's okay to, "Dream On!"

I rented a small apartment on the west side of Indy, and sitting alone inside, I pondered, "What next?" I took any job I could get at the time:

selling cars for a company on the south side. My main objective when I left the military was to pit myself against the chaos of the world and begin to understand who I am in relation to it. To begin to conduct this self-study exercise, I needed a formula, much like a mathematical function that has a rule to resolve it correctly. I soon discovered the art of meditation, which provided a foundation for my self-discovery.

Stress from the military and the transition back into civilian life made me erratic and compulsive; I sought out natural remedies to counter this. Since I didn't like drinking and smoking (and that included doing drugs), meditation sounded harmless. I didn't receive any formal instruction, but purchased books to learn the art. I had an extremely difficult time learning how to meditate. Within 10 minutes into a session, my mind would be all over the place, and often times I'd fall asleep! I made a valiant effort to stick with it, no matter how challenging. Any day off from work, rather than spending my time sleeping in, I'd go to the downtown library to find reading materials on meditation and self-development. One morning at the library, after browsing through so many books, I had still found nothing that captured my attention. Slightly irritated at my failure to find the right book for what I needed, I quit wandering up and down the aisle and sat down at a long and worn wooden table. Sitting lazily, I glanced over to some young people sitting at the table and noticed a small book.

Without picking up the book, I read its title: <u>As a Man Thinketh</u>, by James Allen. The title didn't particularly jump out to me, but there was something about the book that intrigued me. I picked it up and started reading. Already the introduction and first chapters blew my mind! I had never in my life read something so profound and enlightening! I was just a simple kid trying to find his way. I was a marginal student in school and a rebel in the military. If it wasn't a comic book or porn magazine, I wasn't reading it. Yet, it was astonishing to me to read words as beautiful as those in that book, and I wanted more! It's funny to think back at my moments of revelation, sitting there with my mouth wide open; the people sitting at that table must have thought I was insane.

After reading the short book several times, I signed up for a library card and checked it out. The book impressed me so much that I kept it for almost a month. After returning it, I didn't want to read anything else, as I felt an overwhelming urge to start writing. Now, once again, I had never paid attention in my English classes in school. What was I going to write about? I didn't have a clue on how to start, but my plan was simple: pick one thing about myself and methodically dissect the glob of energy that my parents had left me to unravel.

Over the next two to three months, all I did was write. Full of inspiration, every facet of me was met with analysis and deduction of what I did and didn't like.

There would be no stopping me until I had exhausted that specific subject of its meaning (or the lack thereof). I had delineated all of the negatives and prejudices that I'd learned from those who influenced me, including my parents, my grandparents, the military, and the community in which I lived. Often, my deductions were met with anger and tears, yet others with laughter and shame. Each time I would finish exploring a particular issue, I'd go to another, and then another. My goal was to reduce my mind to zero. However, there remained the question in the back of my mind; what is it that I'm trying to achieve? How does this fit into my meditation practices? The answer was staring me in my face. Reflecting on what I learned in Allen's book, I realized that this task was teaching me that more important than focus is control and discipline against the lure of my thoughts. Therefore, the second key to solving my glob of energy was discipline. Armed with new information, I was prepared to take control of my mind, and, in addition to addressing the issues in my mind, two objectives had to be met: I had to instill discipline to protect my new or elevated thought(s) from the negative ones that preceded it, and I had to learn to call on a deeper power within for guidance. Thus, the writing continued, and at each stopping point, I'd began to understand how not to repeat such behavior or emotions by analyzing how discipline fit in and how to meditate, drawing from a deeper source for answers and direction.

Dig deeper

Over time, I began to move on with my life, and I relocated to Las Vegas, Nevada, in search of greater opportunities. This was a great start, and I had a sense that I was going to have fun living in Sin City. However, I used caution to live modestly and not get in over my head indulging in women or gambling.

Within a few months, Lady Luck smiled on me, and I met one of the most awesome women of my life: Veronica. A stunning Filipino from Cebu, Philippines, Veronica came into my life as bold as the very city we lived in. Our romance was like something out of the movies; it was hot, sexy, and fast. From everything Las Vegas presented to us, we enjoyed each bite, and it seemed we could not get enough of Vegas and each other. During this time, I was in love with my life and with this woman, and I just knew we were going to grow old together. However, something I didn't understand about Las Vegas is that it's built on a proverbial house of cards, and fortune and bliss are fleeting. Ergo, my romance with Veronica vanished in just three years, and like a single pull of a dollar slot, it was over. I never saw any warning signs that it was going to end. It just ended. Perhaps there were warning signs that something was wrong with our relationship, but I was blinded by the sway of Las Vegas gambling, drinking, and sex. A combination of the city's wiles and my misstep within my relationship cost me the happiness of being with someone I truly loved. Ironically, Veronica wasn't distracted by the 24-hour dark circus. She cared and nurtured our relationship. I think she had been hoping that I was the man of her dreams, that guy that her parents told her to go find. But, sadly, I didn't live up to my potential as a man, and I sabotaged our relationship. Losing her bothered me for many years, and the one question that weighed heavily on me was, "why didn't I pay attention or put any effort into the relationship?" I didn't have the answers, and I still think of this woman as my soul mate. I felt guilty; Veronica hadn't asked much of me, as she had her own career and money. The only things she requested of me were love and trust. Still tormented, I'm deeply sorry for betraying her love and hope that someday she'll find these words. She left me for someone who seems to be more befitting and attentive to her needs. Perhaps the guy she met wasn't afraid of commitment and was comfortable within his self. I hope he gave her a healthy child and stability and love. I hope he assured her that's he's a true man, someone on whom she could stand and not fall.

On the bright side, Vegas had been good to me – there I had my spiritual breakthrough, and in the strangest setting. Getting off of work a bit early one day, instead of going home, I decided to drive over to a popular west side park, Desert Breeze. The park was vast and had well-manicured soccer fields and a newly built recreation center. I parked off to the side and rolled down my windows for fresh air, and despite the park's busyness, it was exceptionally peaceful. Taking advantage of this tranquil moment, I placed my head back and relaxed into a meditative state. Within my calm disposition, I decided to try a method of seeking answers that I learned from my studies. Earlier in the week, my fiancée and I had hit a rough patch in our relationship. I contemplated our situation and the questions I wanted to ask. However, while I was trying out this new exercise to seek answers, I heard the words, "you're dealing with petty stuff, and there's something far more important for you to experience." While in silence, I didn't fight the urge to question what I had heard and kept the mental pace to see where this was going. At some point, I felt as though I'd gone further than I ever had, and what happened next absolutely astonished me. I witnessed something extremely rare, and there's no amount of money in the world that can purchase it and no level of technology to reach it!

In the darkest and quietest internal space, I felt a veil of some sort lift. It opened up into a pure black void, without a speck of light, not even of the imagination – absolute darkness. Being disciplined, I stayed with the experience and came upon two frozen waterfalls, one to the right and one to the left of me. The waterfall on the left began to shift; it rocked back and forth and flowed into a fade, while the waterfall on the right remained still. Using the boundary from the right water-fall, I peered further beyond it and saw something that I could not perfectly describe in words. I saw, sitting in the center of this universe (my universe), a majestic sphere of energy. It was extremely brilliant, yet not blinding. The powerful presence was enough to drop a person to his or her knees. Although greatly impressive, this whole experience lasted only a few seconds.

As I stared at this unknown force, I heard a voice say, "You are now looking at your subconscious mind." Mesmerized, I remember telling myself, *this moment is extremely rare and witnessed by a privileged few.* Instinctively, I started saying quietly, "I am, I am, I am."

This window into something miraculous closed as fast as it had opened, and there were no words to describe what I had experienced. In fact, not until five or six years later would I share that experience with anyone. Who would believe me? Even more puzzling was the fact that, after I tapped into my inner mind, my third eye also opened. If I had a question about a thing or person and then meditated on it, within 30 minutes I would get a clear vision of the subject and answer to my inquiry. I received answers, direction, and even dialog with some higher voice. For example, wanting to test if I could apply my newfound gift to everyday matters, I inquired as to whether my suspicions were correct about a woman that I was dating and if she had another love interest. Surprisingly, I saw a crystal-clear vision of her having an affair with a red-headed guy with freckles. Curiosity overcame my anger, so I approached her about it. As expected, she denied any affair, but I could see the shock in her face when I gave the details of what her lover looked like. I felt embarrassed and wrong in accusing her, because I could've been wrong, so I didn't press the issue. Ten days later, the guilt had been eating away at her, and she confided in me the truth that she was having an affair. She even gave physical descriptions that matched exactly what I saw in my vision. Sadly, we broke up. Perhaps the thought of having a boyfriend who has psychic powers and can "see" her sneaking around scared her off!

CHAPTER 2

WE'VE BEEN EXPECTING YOU!

IN 2006, I had the opportunity to work for a real estate developer in Williamsburg, Virginia. While driving out of Las Vegas on highway 15 N, I felt mixed emotions; I still cared for my ex-fiancé and didn't want to leave her. As I drove through Utah, my senses had become awakened by the beauty of its countryside. The green grass and vibrant trees were a welcome sight for my eyes, which were accustomed to seeing desert, sand devils, and smog. At long last, I finally arrived in Williamsburg, and my transition was a smooth one. The company that hired me had also given me an incentive package that included a place to stay in one of its corporate condos. When I arrived, I checked in, got my keys, and I crashed, fast asleep, for about 48 hours.

This historical town was impressive. I had not realized that Williamsburg was part of the Historic Triangle of Virginia, which includes Jamestown and Yorktown. As an adult, I had a better appreciation for American history, because this is where America's history all started. The first English settlement and The American Revolutionary War and The siege of Yorktown were real history, right under my feet. Therefore, I made an effort to explore and learn as much as I could about our country's past.

I also have a habit when arriving in any new place to seek out the local bookstores in the area. Within a month of relocating, I had found a small metaphysical book store in New Port News, which is about 35 minutes outside of Williamsburg. The store was quaint and smelled of sage and incense. There wasn't much selection of books, but it was abundant in stones, crystals, jewelry, etc. While browsing through the books, the floor creaked every time I'd move. This constantly caused me to look down out of curiosity. At one point I looked down in amusement and thought to myself, "Surely the owners can get this fixed." As I looked toward my feet, I saw a small paperback book about meditation and nature. I picked it up and was more enthralled by the beautiful cover with a photo of a massive old tree. Intrigued, I purchased it.

Later that afternoon, I decided to spend time at the mall enjoying lemonade and a hot pretzel. With amusement I glanced over at the young boys trying to pick up the cute girls near the food court area. Those poor boys' faces showed such awkwardness as they were rejected by a clique of overly confident young girls. These girls were paying more attention to the task of texting on their cell phones than to the wiles of wobbly legged boys who were grasping their cell phones like a baby clutching its pacifier. Chuckling, I thought to myself, *Man... back in the day it was easy. Now they got to compete with cell phones.*

With about 30 minutes to spare and not wanting to be around the circus atmosphere of the mall, I headed out to the car. The temperature was about 80 with no humidity. Rolling the windows down, I decided to read a few pages from the book with the attractive cover. The paperback was about 90 pages, so it'd take no time for me to read. It was informative on how to meditate, but I considered it to be elementary stuff – great for a beginner.

The Recession

In August 2008, for the first time in my life, I was fired from a job. In my 12 years working for that company, rarely would I miss hitting a sales benchmark. However, reality as it was, I had to be let go. Numbers don't lie, and in the business of sales, success relies on the question of, "What have you done for me lately?"

It felt strange waking up the next morning, having no agenda for the day. Therefore, I had to put together a plan. Because I had enough savings in the bank to get through this rough patch, my first decision was to remain on the east coast and not go back home to Las Vegas. Yet I was concerned about the timing of losing my job. All over the news I heard about the general fear in our nation about an imminent recession, international trade was down, and unemployment began to spike! "This is not good," I remember saying to myself. But I was confident that I could get back on track. After some time, since I couldn't find work in Virginia, I decided to head south.

My plan was to go to Florida and push as hard as I could to find work. What I had not realized is that Florida had been hit hard by the downturn of the economy. I had jumped from the proverbial frying pan into the fire. Not only did I travel throughout Florida searching for work, but I also flew to other states for interviews. In addition, I utilized hiring recruiters and career search websites to further penetrate the job market. At this stage of my search, I had sent out about 250 resumes. Out of that number of resumes, I only secured four interviews, to no avail. Hotel and travel costs were averaging $1,200 per month. Though times had gotten rough; I remained determined.

The economic cloud over America had gotten darker, and everyone, including the wealthy, was scrambling for cover. I prayed daily for protection and that I could find a job opportunity. My bank account was bleeding badly and I started slipping on my bills. The inability to control my finances was sickening, because financial responsibility had always been a priority for me. But with no other options, I knew that some sacrifices had to me made in order to stay afloat. How could anyone survive with no offer or opportunities? To slow the financial hemorrhage, I decided to stop traveling to other states for work and concentrate on work within Orlando. Furthermore, I made the decision to stay at a cheaper hotel that offered weekly rates. Oh God, those places smelled of urine and unwashed bodies. However, it was what I had to do to save some money. In addition, I pawned off anything liquefiable. My debt to income ratio was drastically out of balance at this point, and the collection calls started coming. Helplessly, all I could do was maintain my optimism and keep fighting!

January 2009 came, and my troubles were incessantly shoving me further into a black hole. I had already sent out 400 resumes, and my resolve had become weaker and weaker. Other job sources yielded no results. In addition, I wasted $1100 in fees to recruiting firms. The days were passing, and I canvassed Orlando and Kissimmee and Tampa for any type of work. *This is unbelievable*, I reflected to myself. At every turn checked, every door knocked on, and every stone flipped, there was no job to be had. On one particular night at the hotel, the air was extremely muggy and an unfamiliar smell lingered around that creepy hotel. Wanting to gag, I raced over to Wal-Mart and purchased a $100 air filtration system and some air fresheners. I know I was in no position to splurge, but screw that, that place smelled!

Finally returning to the room and beginning to circulate the air in my room, I decided to meditate. This session was to be a simple exercise with no deeper purpose. While quieting my mind, I reflected on that little book I had purchased a few months back in Virginia. The image of that tree from that book cover stuck in my mind, triggering my memory of some trees that I had admired while working in Virginia. One particular tree with a huge canopy had fascinated me, so I held that image in my mind during meditation. Ten minutes passed, and something bizarre happened; a deep male voice spoke from out of nowhere and said, "We've been expecting you!"

CHAPTER 3

TRANSFORMATION

IT was midnight, and a few days earlier I had been spooked upon hearing that voice during meditation. I couldn't figure out why I had heard those words. There was no logic to any of it, so I dismissed it as mental chatter. To get my mind off that strange experience, I continued to send out resumes on career websites. At this point, my resume count was more than 500, and my outreach spread among the states of California, Nevada, Virginia, Georgia, and Florida. I had to keep focused, because my money was being eaten up with bills, taxes, child support, and traveling costs.

Remarkably, my spirits were still high; however, not receiving any good news, I was beginning to feel the pinch.

At some point, depression set in. I had no appetite and no motivation for life – I mostly just sat in that ugly room. I tried to meditate, but I couldn't control my overwhelming stress and anger over not being able to control my life. A malaise fell over me, and I kept asking - *Why?* I remember visually slipping into confusion, as nothing made sense to me. Sitting for hours with my head on the desk in my room, feeling helpless and dazed, I heard the words come from out of the walls, "Let them take you!", and I immediately heard a snap of the fingers. I awakened to the sound, as if I had been put under hypnosis by a psychiatrist. Startled, I now sought answers as to where these voices were coming from. Is there something going on in this hotel room? I had become so spooked by these strange voices and the thought that someone just might be in there with me, I voiced loudly, "Ain't nobody going to take me nowhere, and if they try, they would get the side of a 6lb steel sledge hammer!"

Entering a deep sleep, I don't remember dreaming. Yet – again! – I awoke suddenly to the snap of fingers. This time when I opened my eyes, standing on the left side of my bed, I saw Jesus Christ! Strangely, I wasn't startled. I remained calm and just looked at him. Smiling, he laid a white sheet over me. There were no words spoken, but I had the feeling that he was saying, "You're going to be okay."

The experience lasted just a few seconds, and I immediately jumped out of bed and raced toward the light switch! "Jesus came to me!" I exclaimed nervously. What did that mean? What was the meaning of the white sheet? I mean, the only time you see white sheets being placed over a body is at the morgue. "Aw…hell naw," I uttered to myself. I remember, as a kid, overhearing a conversation my mom had with one of her friends. She said, "Girl, if you ever saw Jesus for real, that mean you gonna die." So I jumped up and grabbed my hammer, because I wasn't ready to go. Conjuring my thoughts with reason, I meditated on my Jesus sighting. During the silence, the message was that he's protecting and helping me transform. My mind naturally asked the question, *protection from what? And what does transforming mean?* When I focused on those two questions, I saw a flash, and a message appeared to answer to my first question: *The ground of the earth was heavily cracked and desolate. There was a tiny speck of gold on the edge of a precipice, barely enough to barter with. Yet, it was just enough to keep me alive.*

When I woke up, I knew that I had received a blessing of protection with an ominous warning of the potential dangers around me. There were no answers to my second question.

By the third week of February, my savings had dwindled down to a few thousand dollars. My efforts to maintain my insurance, my cell phone bill, food expenses, gas, and hotel lodgings were like nails sealing my coffin shut. The calls for interviews stopped coming in, and the recession was in sixth gear. The money I made from pawning off most of my possessions had already been spent and I struggled to make my truck payments, but maintained insurance on it. It was imperative that I keep my cell phone on, and the largest expense was hotel cost. The months were passing fast, and I was gaining no ground. Therefore, I had to assess my life situation; it had been nine months since I'd lost my job and I've sold or let go of every possession I've owned. My savings dwindled to nothing, and I had zero prospects for work. What was the answer? I wasn't going to make it! Consequently, my only question was, "How am I going to stretch out the money and get through at least the next 90 days?" In order to slow the financial bleeding, I would have to make the toughest decision of my life – to sleep in the truck! The day of checkout, I took as many towels and toiletries that I could get my hands on. I wasn't sure how this was going to work out, but it was a decision I had to make.

Luckily, it was the time of year where the temperature is pleasant, because I'd heard the summers in Florida can be rough. At least I had that going for me. But there was one important factor, and that was conserving gas, especially when the prices were at $2.75 per gallon. Therefore, I drove as little as possible and often went to the mall to keep cool. Because of my military background, I had planned efficiently how I was going to live in that truck and how to maintain hygiene. It was imperative that I kept myself up, because my job search was priority one!

I chose to stay in Orlando, because it had the most hotels that would fit my plan. My #1 rule was never to show in my expression or appearance that I was homeless. Therefore, prior to checking out of that hotel earlier in week, I took all of my laundered shirts and pants for business to the dry cleaners. Those items stayed hung in my truck – no wrinkling. Also, I wore mostly flip flops and loose gym pants and tops, while my casual wear was folded and neatly packed away. Ultimately, if I got a job interview, I would be ready. During the night, I would drive around and find a hotel with the most cars in its parking lot. I purposely made sure not to park alone or in a dark area, because this would attract security. I would find a parking space in a populated area and pull in between two vacationer's vehicles. I had a shade for the main wind shield, and the driver and passenger windows were tinted, so no one could see in. The back window was blocked with two hanging garment bags. A person would have to go out of his or her way to look in from the rear.

I blended in perfectly and only ran my truck when necessary for air conditioning. Every morning presented a challenge regarding how to maintain hygiene. I got up from 6:00-7:00 a.m.; there's not much activity at that time. I would slip on my Nike gym pants and shirt and hat to look like a tourist. I carried nothing on my person, except my wallet. Once I had located the side or rear hotel doors, I'd casually walk in like I was staying there. Not wasting any time, I gave myself exactly three minutes to go into the bathroom, spot clean myself, and get out. When I got back to the truck, I would brush my teeth with bottled water. Fresh and "street cleaned," after my morning routine and a meal of a McDonald's breakfast burrito, I would drive somewhere with shade and continue my job search. I had my laptop and cell phone, my two imperative items for communication with potential employers. The laptop had a wireless card that proved to be invaluable anywhere I went.

At this point, my ego had taken a back seat with regard to what type of work I could find. In 10 days, I had applied to six major retail and wholesale outlets, five car dealerships, five retail pharmacies, three hotel Janitor positions, and other labor jobs.

Going on 12 days of sleeping in the truck, I wasn't feeling very good about myself. Any motivation I had to look for work was being worn down. One night, highly upset by my situation of being financially wiped out, I dug through my bag and pulled out my favorite white Bible, which had been given to me by my brother, Phil. That Bible had been in my possession since May 25, 1983, and has traveled with me all over the world. After 30 minutes of reading passages from Psalms and Matthews, the Florida humidity lulled me to sleep. Around 3:00 a.m., I woke up in heavy mugginess and turned on the air condition for about 10 minutes to cool things down. Shifting about the truck to get comfortable, I reached over from the passenger side to turn off the ignition and to remove the windshield shade and noticed how a nearby street light strangely casted its yellow shadows across the trees below it.

In a deep slumber, a familiar smell of skillet fried corned beef hash with Vidalia onions and eggs permeated my senses. I could almost taste cheese grits with butter and sugar! The only person in my life that cooked this type of food was my mom, and that's exactly who was coming through my spiritual channel. I guess she figured that seeing Jesus standing over me with a sheet was a bit too dramatic for me, so she used a simpler and more inviting approach – food!

My mom's name was Sandra, and sadly, she had succumbed to cancer in April 2001. Mom was a firecracker of a personality. A jersey girl, she had a certain snap that is unique only to those born in the New York/New Jersey area. Predominately English and Irish in her blood, with a low percentage of African-American roots, she could have passed for Italian, Greek, or Spanish. She had quick intelligence, and at times her personality was like Mercury – you couldn't grasp it. What I loved most about her was that she could go from zero to steaming mad in about three seconds flat. On the turn of a dime she could recognize humility and be most congenial to all. When I saw Mom, she was coming through some portal of white light, like a friend who was just stopping by, having been in the neighborhood. She was accompanied by ten to twelve souls who had come by to check on me. She and the others were in pure energy form, yet a slight black outline of their bodies gave definition. Upon seeing her in my vision, I started crying. We walked into a small house with a single room for privacy. I apologized to her for my crying, and she responded, "Its ok for boys to cry for their mothers, sit here." Mom sat to the right of me, and said, "I realize that you're going through a difficult time, but I want you to remember what I always told you when you used to sit on those stairs in our home. Even if it seems too dark, there's always light to be found. So, keep on your path of the straight and narrow – you will find light." Listening intently, the same way I did at 13 years old, I heard her say with that Jersey snap, showing that she's still the boss, "I am sending you a woman who'll be in my image; but remember, I'm your momma… she ain't."

Our conversation ended just as fast as it began. We both stood up, and I hugged her in a way that only a son could. I stood in the door of that little house and saw her rejoin the other souls waiting for her.

Though I was still sleeping, I could feel myself actually laughing, because one of the bright souls had the outline of a tall and handsome man with wavy hair like Clark Gable – my mom always loved tall and handsome men! He took her took her by the hand; she smiled and stepped into the White portal of light.

I woke up from my sleep and discovered that I had been crying! My shirt lapel was mildly wet and my cheeks were moist. Then something amazing happened; I automatically rolled down my window for air, instinctively looked out toward the city-lit sky, and heard my mother's voice distantly say, "Off to have a good time, dear!"

Back to the basics

All day, I contemplated the message from my mom, which was to follow the path of the straight and narrow. That meant I must continue my passion to explore and discover who I am through the discipline of meditation. In addition, I'd been on this course of self-resolution for 15 years. The conclusion is that I had the tools to begin to change my situation, so my first task was to get myself out of that truck and into better sleeping quarters. It took me exactly 14 days to go from sleeping in my truck to staying in a luxury condominium. Now, at first I didn't know if my plan was going to work, because I was careful not to get caught up in wishful thinking. A person can pray until blue in the face and bang their head against a brick wall, but unless the right conditions are present to support the desire, nothing will happen. Supporting conditions that lead a person toward manifestation can swing both ways and serve equally the corrupted and evil people in the world. How many times have you heard people say that while they are struggling, they can't understand why a vile person is getting their way easily in life? The answer is simple, if their supporting conditions (people, ideas, things, and themselves) are in order within that specific experience, then manifestations arises.

In the face of uncertainty, I had to try. I had to see if I was in perfect timing with elements seen and unseen. All I had was faith that

I could do it. My job search was a bigger challenge for me to manifest; the supporting conditions weren't there for any job opportunity to be offered. Consequently, I focused on something that I could create: an opportunity to get out of that truck! I released myself from worry and realigned my intention to have better living arrangements. In addition, I became balanced with Nature through meditation. That afternoon, I immediately dropped all worries of being unemployed. However difficult, I began to catch any and all thoughts and fears about my situation and negate them. Next, I put together an affirmation plan that included downloaded a picture of a luxury condo loaded with all of the comforts and pen and pad. My goal was, within 14 days, to live in a beautiful and warm condo while surrounded with well-groomed landscaping with plenty of sunlight. The plan of action called for me to write out on piece of paper and on each line my deepest desire to live in a safe and beautiful condo. There was no room for weakness, as I had to be extremely discipline to my affirmation. My passion was to fill each line on that tablet and complete upwards of five full sheets per day.

Within a few days, it was clear to me what I wanted. Also, I was in sync with nature and began to receive signals or signs to start going to church and the way will be further opened. Around the fourth day of my goal routine, I almost disrupted the flow. I started losing focus due to the daily irritations of living in that truck and the hunger I felt. My agitation was perpetuated when I rationed myself only $10 per day for food. Once, distracted, I accidentally smashed my finger on the back hatch of the truck. That was an immediate signal from Nature – a painful one – that I'm about to change course. Recognizing this, I got back into the discipline of creating what I wanted.

Following the instructions of my inner voice, I randomly picked a non-denominational church on the east side of Orlando in a community called Winter Park. Services were held at least twice per week, and I would always sit in the back. Always well groomed, no one would have known my station in life just by looking at me. I committed to going to that church until something materialized for me. After about a week of attending services and enjoying the music and positive energy, I began to recognize the regulars. One old black man stood out in my mind more than the rest. He was in his 70s and was a sharp dresser. He reminded me of my late great-grandfather, Dr. Wilmoth Baker, whom always presented himself with class. Likewise, the old man was cut from the same cloth of a long-ago era, when a smart-looking brim, three-pleated slacks, and polished Stacy Adams were the norm. The old man is part of a classy society of men who are now being overshadowed by wannabes' who dare to go out in public with pajamas and rubber sleepers with big holes. I noticed that he wore a Buffalo Soldiers pin on his coat lapel, which caught my attention due to my affinity for American history.

One evening, the old man and I pulled into the church parking lot at the same time. Noticing each other, I offered the first greeting and handshake, saying, "My name is Chris. "

"Hello Chris. I'm Mr. Bradford. I've noticed you're new to our church," he replied.

"Yes sir… been coming for about a week now." Looking at his pin, I asked, "Did you have a relative that served with the Buffalo Soldiers?"

Impressed that any young person would recognize the symbol, let alone know anything about this famous fighting group, he said, "As a matter of fact, my grandfather served with them!"

Wanting to display what little knowledge I had of the Buffalo Soldiers, I chimed in, "Their history and bravery is awesome. Which did he serve, the 10th or 24th Cavalry Regiment?"

"He served in the 10th Calvary Regiment," he said, looking at me, impressed. "It looks like you know your history."

"Well sir, I don't know much, but I learned the origin of its name and the two legends that surround it. One is that the name "Buffalo Soldier" was given to them by the Cheyenne Indians, meaning "wild buffalo," and as the other legend has it, the founder of the 10th Regiment, Colonel Grierson, gave them that name because of their ferocious fighting skills against the Comanche Tribe." I had whipped that knowledge on him all before we hit the front porch of that church.

The old man just looked at me proudly. "You're all right. Thank you for taking the time to know our history as black men!"

We walked in and sat in our respective places. The service went fast that night, yet, it was still the same 1½-hour schedule. After the service, while walking out to my truck, the old man caught up to me. "Young man, what are you getting ready to do?"

"Nothing... just heading back home." Of course, he didn't know that I was homeless, yet I had to say something normal. "What's up?" I asked.

"If you're not doing anything, come with me up the street for a bite to eat – my dime!" Mr. Bradford said.

Of course, I wasn't about to refuse. I really didn't have anything to do. He looked level headed and I didn't think he's try no funny stuff. Besides, it's a free meal! "Sure, Mr. Bradford, that sounds great."

We went to a local favorite, Fiddler's Green Irish Pub and Eatery. With a down-to-earth atmosphere, I liked the establishment as soon as we entered. The service was prompt, and both Mr. Bradford and I wasted no time ordering. This one thing about us guys is that we're not much for chatter – we just want to eat!

After the waitress brought our drinks, Mr. Bradford asked me to tell him about myself. There wasn't much to say, and I really wasn't comfortable telling my story to a stranger. "Well, there's not much to the story, other than having served a short stint in the military and most of my career has been in the real estate industry. I was married once, and we had two boys. But mostly my focus in life has been my career."

With a look in his eyes, as if he knew something I didn't, he asked, "How long have you been in Orlando?"

"Oh... just a few months," I responded awkwardly. "Have you lived here long?" I asked, trying to turn the conversation on him.

"Yeah, I've lived here almost 40 years!" said the old man.

"You've definitely seen this place grow, huh?" I could see that something was stirring in the back of Mr. Bradford's mind.

Yep," he said with a snap, "I'm curious, and not that's any issue, what brought you to our church?"

"I don't know. The other night I was praying on something and I received a message to go to church." I shrugged my shoulders, "I didn't know where to go, so I picked this one."

Our food arrived. I had ordered corned beef and cabbage, and Mr. Bradford ordered a salmon dish. Yum, I can still taste it now! While we dug our forks into the fare, Mr. Bradford asked, "Wanna hear a story?"

"Sure!" I replied while gobbling down a mouthful of cabbage.

"When I was 30-something, I had just gotten out of the Navy. I was up in Jacksonville for a while. Anyway, I got out and met this girl, and you know how it goes... we fell in love."

I continued listening, not missing a beat with the corned beef.

"So we came down here to Orlando to begin a new life. I found a job working in a kitchen at a hotel making $147 per month," the old man related.

I almost choked when he said that.

Continuing, he said, "Life was good, and my girl, she had a job too. We were planning to get married and talked about a home for the future. So we started saving our money. Now remember, even though $150 doesn't sound like a lot of money now, back then a buck was worth something. We saved for about two years until that tramp took all the money and ran off to New York with some long-toothed Puerto Rican fellow."

I started laughing and asked, "How much did she get you for?"

"That ho took $300!" Mr. Bradford says with a dark look in his eye.

"Did you ever get it back?" I asked, keeping pace with my fork.

"Nah, didn't need to. Come to find out she was trying to run the fast life, and that guy she went up there with strung her out on heroin and died. That whole situation didn't make a sense – poor girl."

"Dang, that's crazy," I said.

Taking a couple of bites and washing it down with a lager, he said, "Yeah, that wasn't a good time, because when she took that money, it put me in a bind. I didn't have money for rent and ended up sleeping at my brother's house, and he had a wife and six crumb snatchers." He chuckled, as if he had been with them yesterday.

I laughed too, because I couldn't imagine living with all those people under one roof.

Mr. Bradford continued. "I tried to adapt, but I couldn't do it. It was too many people trying to live in that tiny house. My brother had this old, ugly '55 Buick in the backyard. I told him I'd sleep in that thing."

"Did the car run?" I asked curiously.

"Yeah, but it smoked something terrible. Because my brother had another newer Buick out front, it was rarely driven."

Taking another gulp of his beer, he said, "Well, what turned out to be a temporary thing ended up to be two months living in that uncomfortable wreck. But I got a lucky break. I found a job working and cleaning a butcher shop. Real nice old man owned the place – Jewish fella'. He taught me the ropes on cutting meat and how to run a business and let me stay upstairs in a converted attic. Now, it exactly wasn't the Waldorf Astoria, but it beat sleeping in that dry rotting bucket."

I was amused listening and watching Mr. Bradford reflect on his past.

"You know, that old man treated me like his own son, and he eventually sold his business to me," Mr. Bradford said with a distant look in his eye. "I kept that meat shop for 20 years until I retired."

Then Mr. Bradford's countenance switched from that of a reminiscing old man to that of a father, "Do you know why I told you that story?"

"No sir."

The old man leaned across the table and lowered his voice. "Because I know that you are homeless and sleeping in your truck!"

I almost coughed up my meal! There was no way to hide the fact that he was right. Embarrassed, I asked, "How do you know?"

"I know from experience. I basically lived out of that car for two months and didn't have any place to go and no money to move about. But most of all, I know that look in a man's eyes. It's a look that only a man who's been there can recognize."

Still curious as to how he knew that I was living out of my truck, I asked, "What's that look?"

Fixing his napkin in his lap and raising his chin. "It's the look of deep despair, hidden by pride and determination. The eyes don't lie, Son!"

"Yes, sir, you're right" I responded sheepishly.

"I tell you what: because of my good fortune and in-kind gesture to the old man who helped me to find my way, I tell you what I'm going to do. I own a second home in Lake Mary, and you can stay there for one month to 45 days until my grandchildren come down for the summer. Will that work?" asked the kind old man.

While tears began to well up, I fought hard to not show my emotion. Sensitive to my position, Mr. Bradford didn't want me to feel awkward and changed the subject. However, he reminded me that, when our meal was over, he'd give me the directions and keys to the place.

We finished our meal and chatted for a bit more, and Mr. Bradford said that we should get going, because he wanted to get home to watch his recording of American Idol. Chuckling to myself, I thought, *this old dude is cool.*

Lake Mary was further north on I-4, a small community with a population of 15,000 residents. I loved the sprawling land that each homeowner had. We drove through winding roads and passed lakes. I was beginning to like this place already. We finally got to his home and it was *gorgeous*. White with a new-looking brown roof, the house looked like it had been built less than 10 years ago. His landscaping was meticulous – three palm trees stood in the front yard with warm lights strung up their trunks.

Mr. Bradford gave me a quick tour and flipped the keys over to me. "We'll talk later in the week, and don't worry about a thing. Good night."

I didn't know what to say with that emotional lump in my throat. "Thank you."

"Any kid who knows about the Buffalo Soldiers is a friend of mine. Goodnight." Mr. Bradford walked out the door, and I dropped to my knees in thankful prayer and gratitude that God had granted my wish to get off the streets.

CHAPTER 4

CONTACT

BECAUSE of the stress I had endured for 10 months fighting out in the world, surviving, and traveling and had basically lost, I had to heal. Momentarily, I didn't worry about finding work, because I had friends from out of state that assisted me financially. To reintegrate socially, I found a local self-help group through a network called Meet Ups! There would be several of these social groups I would attend. Some were metaphysical, and others would be literary. I went to one group, and the subject was Remote Viewing. Now, I had never heard of that term; however, apparently it's been around for quite some time. Remote Viewing is the ability to see "targets" and/ or gather information about a thing, person, or target. While I was listening to the speaker about the subject, the question came to me, *am I doing this*?

One evening, I went to a group session where the subject was about whether there were other intelligences in the universe? There were about 20 people attending that evening. Parts of the conversation were lively and intelligent, while others were just plain silly. One of the participants, a young college student, had mentioned her fascination with the possibility of life existing near the star Vega, the brightest star in the Constellation Lyre. I'd heard this suggestion before, mostly in literary fiction works. Even though she admitted that a lot of this belief is based in fiction, she pointed out that a lot of the books and movies made are written by credible sources in the business of space and science. These smart people of science are dreamers, just like the average man. If a scientist, who has access to advanced information and machines, dares to dream about life around Vega, perhaps they see something we don't.

There may be some truth in what that young lady said. For me, she made a valid point. This world is too complex and magnificent to be the only one hosting intelligence. In addition, just because science hasn't been able to unravel the universe's mysteries or at least explain it in terms they can understand, that doesn't mean intelligent life doesn't exist elsewhere. Often times, when the unexplainable can't be deduced to reason and logic, we will then place it in the categories of fiction, folklore, and fables simply because we don't understand it fully.

The Contact!

On the way home from the workshop that night, I pondered on whether I could make a connection with an alien life form. After all, I do have a gift to tap into the subconscious mind and connect with any person or thing – why not an alien? Still reasoning, I thought that, if within everyone sits the subconscious mind, which is a fragment of the larger universal mind, and there's the wide belief that all life is intricately connected, then why not see if I can make a connection? Now, one issue I had was how to introduce my inquiry about something that is conjecture. As an optimist, I came to the conclusion that I should create a mental template. This was needed because, unlike a personal subject or something tangible or intangible yet verifiable, going on conjecture was not only risky, but would also cause me to lose focus. The template would only be used as an introduction (a teaser), not to lay the groundwork or set the precedence built on illusion. I thought about the young lady's argument about the possibility of life near the star Vega. Therefore, I went online to see what this star looked like and learned as much information about its planetary system as I could. Over the next hour, I formulated my mental template of what I thought Vega's planetary system looked like, including the heavy dust particles surrounding it.

In the back of my mind, I had many questions: *What if? What will happen? Am I prepared if I do make contact?* I had many questions, but

I had to keep focused. I stuck with my mental picture of this planetary system with the large blue/white star. Dust particles and rocky-looking planets slowly rotated counter clockwise. The process was slow, because my mind kept drifting, and I would not move on to the next step until I demonstrated consistency. Once my concentration on the template stabilized, I immediately released it and began to meditate deeply. My breathing was very shallow and deliberate. Next, when my mind was clear, I began to place my attention near the location of the subconscious mind (midway between the sternum and navel). I held that position for almost 10 minutes. Like a space shuttle releasing its booster rockets and the craft ascends deeper, I felt an emotional shift and went deeper to another level of consciousness. This next step is the tricky part. I was at the place where consciousness and unconsciousness meet. On some occasions, this is the point at which I would fall asleep. Here it's easy to forget what you are doing and where you are. Holding my attention at the crossroads was crucial. I introduced my intention (the Vega template) at the center where the inner two worlds meet and hold. The trick to holding is to introduce the subject, let go, and wait! It's not to hold with expectation or becoming fixated on getting results, but it's about holding with patience.

I was at the crossroads of where reality and phenomenon meet, and I kept introducing my mental template very lightly, just enough to cause a spark. I would only introduce the image for about 10 seconds or so, and then back off. Remember, I was in perfect suspension internally, careful to not upset the balance. I teased the subconscious about a total of 4-5 times. The next time I presented the template, I felt a mental shift! This shift felt like when a car is put into low transfer and torque can be felt. When that experience happened, the unexplainable continued. It felt like my mind or thoughts skipped! Similar to a rock skipping on water, my mind (more like frequency) skipped beyond the Vega template I introduced. The template had vanished. A part of me was getting worried, but I told myself to stay the course. When that skipping motion took place, my inner vision came alive. I was traveling fast, through murky-colored rolls of cloud or fog. My body had a heightened sense of awareness that something imminent was about to unfold. Still traveling through some brownish-black-colored fog, a clear hole emerged, about the size of a tea cup plate, and it opened! Surveying the opening and to my utter shock, I saw the left profile of a young female from the neck up, with a small nose and warm-looking eyes. Her facial features were delicate, similar to those of a young Asian girl. Her skin color was white with a hint of grey. My mind quickly thought, *This is nothing like anything I've seen before; she looks different!* Realizing that someone has just looked in on her, she gasped with shock, and immediately covered the hole in her space with her hand. Abruptly, I ended the viewing and was rocked as to what I had just seen. Was that real? Did I see it? My mind raced, and my heart was beating rapidly, laced with caution.

Startled by what I had just seen, I laid down to calm myself. Not only was the experience un-nerving, but the energy could not be explained. Psychically, I must have remained connected to whatever I tapped into, because when I lay down with my eyes still open, I could see that I was still there. It was like I was in two worlds, conscious of both at the same time. To be honest, an uncomfortable feeling came over me as to what I had done. I was paralyzed with fear – literally. Still connected to this other world, I stood outside what looked like a basic small house. There was a warm globe of yellowish-brown light hovering and motioning me to follow it. I followed it into the empty house. When I walked in, I saw a very tall and skinny entity (a male energy), about 9 feet tall or more. I couldn't make out his features, but his skin was brown to black, and he had very large hands. Demonstrating his strength and with his back to the wall, he lifted a full-grown human male by the top of his head with one hand and held it at chest level. Continuing to follow this light, I walked past this demonstration off to my right and walked out into the backyard. The light faded. I stood; I next was met with a military leader. He was about 7 feet tall, and his body looked like it was made of black armor. His face was symmetrical, like stealth armor. This military figure smiled and gestured for me to follow him to a subterranean level. As I followed, he had soldier-like entities to the right and left of us, similar to our military Pass and Review ceremony. Then I became really frightened as we entered a subterranean clearing that was illuminated by red-hot rocky walls. What was strange, unlike a descent by stairs or an elevator, it felt like we were going from one dimension into another. My mind was on overload, and I forced myself to wake. Still with my eyes wide open and like someone was peering through the glass at me, I saw that military figure's face smiling creepily at me. I was so upset and angry at myself for having done what I had that I did not attempt another viewing of any kind for nine months!

CHAPTER 5

THIS IS WHAT YOU SEEK

FALL 2009 had come, and it'd been since May that I'd made first contact. But contact with what and where? Was it real? The self-inquiries and debates were too much to handle. Although I cut off any behavior related to viewing, I can feel something resonating deep within my soul. It was a psychological tug of war. However, I fought it and suppressed that memory every time it began to rise.

There was still the issue of surviving and somehow getting work. I did find a commission-only opportunity for a startup company selling leads, yet I was in no shape to sell on commission. Consequently, I left within the first week to find something solid. However, it seemed that, during my employment search - the words *jobs* and *guaranteed* were no longer synonymous. I did find a job posting for the U.S. Postal Service in Gainesville, Florida. I went through all of the testing requirements, passed, and was instructed to arrive on a specific date for interviewing. Arriving to Gainesville as instructed, I saw a line outside the postal building door that looked like a soup kitchen line. I asked a guy who was waiting, "Is this line for postal customers or the job interview?"

"Job Interview," said the 40-something, unshaved, skinny white guy.

Unbelievable, I thought to myself. Eventually, they let everyone in and directed us to a conference room. Right away, a supervisor greeted us. Without wasting time, he told us that the postal service was cutting back and losing jobs. I thought to myself, *then what are we doing here?*

He went on to say that the position offered would only be part-time and temporary, meaning one day per week! Like a cow being prodded and causing a stampede with 50 others trying to get out of the way, that conference room cleared in 30 seconds, with me leading the way. This had turned out to be another disappointment.

I'd never been much for horoscopes, but I wanted to get side bar information as to what was going on in my life. So, while eating a burger, I pulled out my laptop and typed in my birth sign – Virgo. The search results brought up articles about Saturn in Virgo and lasting a few years. I didn't understand one word of it, but all I know is that Saturn had been beating Virgos (especially this one!) to a pulp. I needed to read something more positive and specific, like, "Chris, this is your lucky day; you will be called by your former employer, and they'll offer your job back – with back pay!" Ok, I know that was a bit much to expect, but that's what I needed to read, not, "You must be closer to the soil and pay attention to the simpler things in life." If I hadn't paid $1200 for that laptop, I would have punched that online astrology information in its pixel. *Wow*, I thought, *I'm already homeless, how much closer to the ground does this Saturn guy wants me to be?*

My season in Florida was up; I'd exhausted all means and efforts to survive there. However, there was bright side to moving away from Florida; I had found an opportunity to work at the Youth Academy on the Ft. Stewart military base in Hinesville, Ga. (Unfortunately, I already didn't like the sound of that town. In anyplace with "ville" in its name, you know it has to be back woods!). I said good bye to Mr. Bradford, who'd been like a guardian angel and mentor to me. Orlando was rough; however, I had experienced much: hotels, job hunting, Mr. Bradford, kind strangers, and having contact with an alien!

I was looking forward to going to Georgia, as I have a good friend who lives in Atlanta. In light of our friendship that spanned more than 20 years, if I didn't stop by his home, then it would be an insult to our prior military camaraderie. I arrived to Tyrone's home a few weeks before Christmas and enjoyed the warmth, people, music, and good food there. My head had been buried in stress for over a year; therefore,

I felt that it was okay to let my guard down and enjoy the holidays. A few days after Christmas, after the liquored fog of the egg nog had worn off, I called the Youth Academy that had offering me the job to be a member of their cadre. I was supposed to report on January 5, 2010. Yet when I called to ask about something else, a lady in personnel stated that there'd been a delay and that I should not come down; someone will follow up with me soon. The high I had from the Christmas reveling and happiness had been taken down a notch. I wanted to ask the reason for the delay, but having worked for the government I realized that civil service personnel are unfairly mean, so I kept my mouth shut. With this unexpected delay and momentarily no place to stay, I asked my friend if I could borrow the downstairs couch a little while longer. He was cool with it, even though I felt awkward in my position, not wanting to wear out my welcome. I tried to maintain face that my world was okay, yet it really wasn't.

On New Year's, Tyrone and his family went all out! A limousine and champagne and Hennessy (top shelf) were the staples of ringing in 2010 right! There were about 15 of us, and it was a blast! 3...2...1... Happy New Year! Everyone was cheering and hugging, but my heart was extremely heavy, because so many people had been depending on me in the past year and a half, and I had let them down. I'd defaulted on all of my financial obligations. My savings and investment accounts were depleted. I'd wasted paper by sending out 600 resumes. I'd spent over $6,500 traveling in my search for work. My younger brothers and sisters needed help. The cold hard fact was that, at the turn of 2010, I did not recognize myself anymore.

On January 4, I still hadn't heard anything from my contact at the academy. I called and got no response. However, I did receive an email on the issue, stating that hiring had been temporarily suspended and would be opened back up around the third week of January. Weeks prior, when the personnel lady had told to me that there'd been an operational hiring change, I knew I wasn't going to get the position. After discussing this with Tyrone, he suggested that I just go on down to Hinesville and see what's going on and perhaps to check out other opportunities as well. Knowing my living situation, he made the transition easier and offered me use of their second home there, (Tyrone used to be stationed at Ft. Stewart and had purchased this home back in the 90s). I arrived in Hinesville, Ga., during the third week of January. Coincidentally, the email alert on my phone signaled a message from the Youth Academy operations. The email instructed me to come for an interview on February 9.

On the day of the interview, I prepared myself and prayed that this would be a good opportunity for me. All traffic had to enter the main gate off of General Screven road, and all non-military personnel had to be issued a one-day day pass to enter the base. Seeing those young men and women conducting their business with seriousness caused me to reflect on my years in the military. I could appreciate the tediousness and attention to detail that must be given when there are thousands of cars coming and going daily. The Youth Academy was at the rear of the base, and along the way, I passed Stryker infantry vehicles, mean-looking Humvees, and big bad-ass artillery guns. I even saw some kid run out of a chow hall and puke all over the grass. *Yep, I'm on an Army base*, I said to myself.

Arriving at the academy on time, I proceeded directly to operations. There were young cadets logging the entry of all persons entering the building. With their young baby faces and bursting potential, they were there at the behest of the state. The young men and women there had some type of criminal background or other infarction. Consequently, the academy was a place for them to grow, be educated, and learn how to be contributive to society, rather than becoming a liability, or worse – a prisoner. I thought to myself, *I hope these two young men make it in life*. After filling out documents, I waited for about 20 minutes for the commandant of the school. The commandant, a retired military veteran, was an older man of Latin origin. After we exchanged few pleasantries, the meeting was shorter than the total wait time to see him. The firm-faced commandant looked over my resume and asked a few questions, my answers to which I think satisfied him. He explained that the opportunity I was there for was a part-time assignment, and because of state cutbacks, he could not guarantee me more than 29 hours per week. Personally, I didn't mind; this was the most I'd gotten out of anyone in my entire job search. But then he said the word, "however…." I knew what was coming, and my face fell.

"However, because I have a full staff with seniority, I really need a part-time cadre member for about one day per week. It could change as time goes on, yet there may be times I may not need you for a month." To nail this coffin even tighter, the commandant concluded his statement with, "Keep your other options open."

Honestly, I didn't know how much more a man could take, but I maintained face, thanked him for the opportunity, and refused his offer. Why would I say yes to that? It would cost me money to work for them. The irritation of not being able to put together any string of good luck for myself of finding a job was beginning to wear thin. Living in Georgia brought no more positive experience than living in Florida had. While contemplating my past experience in Florida, I remembered a message I had received while staying in that hotel, "Let them take you." Then I thought, *I wonder if that contact I made with that alien last June has anything to do with that message.*

Re- contact in March 2010

Since nothing in my life was working, and trying to stay open minded to explore that specific message, I decided to re- contact that female entity and see where it led. When I released the mental hold that was in place for nine months, my body felt a long chill. Re-enacting the methods that allowed me to make successful contact earlier, this time the connection was forged faster. Having a successful link, the feeling is balanced and the energy around the subject is unobstructed and feels alive. So when I emitted my signal, the connection to that place and to that female entity was instant.

My vision began to clear. I saw myself and the smaller female entity in black robes, staring at each other while standing on a narrow dirt road. To the right of us I could see that the sky was a translucent medium purple. Seeing that, I knew that was not the atmosphere of Earth. To our right was a wooden fence that served as a barrier for the tallest wheat fields I'd ever seen. In the backdrop of this wheat field was an old brown barn. However, it was not abandoned, and the energy around it felt warm. While I was seeing this from a higher vision, I wondered, *why we are wearing black robes?* Then I understood; we were respecting each other's bodies. In addition, the robes made it easier for me to maintain contact without becoming frightened. We were both looking at each other in amazement, yet I could barely see her face for the hood draping over it. I wasn't afraid when she grabbed my hand and led me into the towering wheat plants. Walking slowly, she said, "This is what you seek." I knew immediately what she meant, because ever since I lost my job and life, all I had prayed for was abundance, growth, and stability!

Engineering

The viewing of her and me in that wheat field switched to a familiar location – my own living room. Still in a trance-like state, everything in my mind turned to black, and then a blank piece of paper appeared. I looked at the blank paper and saw a pencil begin to sketch a figure of a dark brown-skinned woman with long black hair who wore tribal ornaments and necklaces.

"What is this?" I asked with curiosity.

"We engineered the brown-skinned people on your planet," the alien said, still cloaked.

"What?" I yelled.

"We engineered the brown people in your Western hemisphere," she responded.

I was having a hard time concentrating during this contact, because without any introduction, she slammed me with this information that they had engineered brown-skinned people. Although I wanted to hear more, the alien quickly ended our communication and motioned to me to sleep and said that we'd talk later. When the experience ended, I found myself in a daze, and I just stared at the ceiling.

At about 12:30 a.m., I couldn't sleep at all. There was so much to contemplate, but there was nowhere to start. Also, I didn't know who this female was or what she fully looked like. There was no way to logically process the information that some aliens engineered a whole race of people! I decided to start taking notes to try to see where this was going.

CHAPTER 6

XZABEA

THE following night, I couldn't wait to re-establish connection with this entity. Viewing is easier to do at night, because the body naturally sedates to sleep; in this way I don't have to concentrate as hard as I would during the day when physical and mental energies are high. At about 11:30 p.m., I lay down to begin my connection. It only took about 15-20 minutes to make a connection. The same female immediately appeared, standing in a doorway. This doorway looked somewhat familiar. I could almost make out the outline of her body, but her appearance was still hazy. From what I could tell, she was small with a fragile frame. If I were to guess, her height was around 5 feet. One thing was for sure: she didn't look like those aliens they show on television, with the monstrous heads and tiny bodies. Although I could only see her outline, her body looked in well proportion according to human standards.

"Hi Chris, remember me?" she asked exuberantly.

The way she asked the question felt like we had some past relationship. I didn't respond because I stared in disbelief at the ugly little male creature standing next to her. This thing was short and dumpy. His nose was small, yet jagged at the nostrils, and he looked like a deranged little pig. There was also a hunch-backed creature behind her, creeping around curiously. I screamed at the top of my lungs. "NO! No way does he come along. Get out!" The alien immediately cut contact so that I wouldn't go into shock. Just as the previous bizarre episode, I was unable to process mentally what was going on and wrote this event in my journal. I fell back to sleep without incident.

A few days later, I followed up on part 2 of a multi-step process to join the Cobb County Sheriff's Dept., in Atlanta. The drive from Hinesville to Atlanta is about 4½ hours. Tyrone swears he does it in 3½ (yeah right). I arrived at 8:00 a.m., but was too physically and mentally stressed for any testing that day. All I wanted to do is sleep. The first phase was a written test that had been administered two weeks earlier, which I passed. This second phase was the obstacle course and review of the sworn application.

Cold wind blew furiously, the threat of rain hovered in the clouds, and all the candidates were escorted by the sheriff's personnel to the obstacle course. The staff gave instructions on how to navigate the course, which would be timed. People from all walks of life were vying for a few sheriff positions. Young men, single mothers, middle-aged women, fat ex-military guys, and one skinny bro (me), who really didn't have the desire to join the police department. I was the second candidate to run the obstacle course. Having not slept the night prior and legs wobbly from the long drive, my energy level was at less than 50% power.

"Lee!" yelled one of the instructors, "whenever you're ready!" That was my queue to run. I was jumping, running, balancing, and maneuvering like I was 19 years old. The last obstacle was a long, 15' cement tube that I had to crawl through. The opening was about 36" wide, so it was tight. I shot through that tube like a bullet; however, upon exiting the cement tube, caution was yelled out by one of the instructors to not hit my head on the hard edge. Therefore, I gave myself about ½ second longer to come up. I blasted out that tube and was still in a crouched position. I couldn't get my fatigued legs underneath me to balance the momentum, and I began to topple. Going over head first, I fell and rolled around like a mad monkey playing in mud. Feeling stupid, I quickly got up and crossed the finish line in good time. The next 30 minutes were spent cheering and motivating the other candidates to get over those obstacles in good time.

There was a very sexy, middle-aged brunette also competing for one of the sheriff position. While at the obstacle course, I kept laughing to myself, as it soon became apparent that the girl had not an athletic bone in her body. Though she was fit, she had clearly led a cream-and-silk lifestyle. Determination was set in her eyes, and when the instructor yelled out her name to run, she took off as if it were the last run of her life. The first obstacle was a six-foot wall, and the goal was to run up, scale over it, and keep going. Well, when the brunette attacked it, I heard a loud, "thunk"; she had slammed right into it like a bug! Then she stuck to the wall and didn't move. It was as if Velcro was holding her up. I heard only sounds of her whimpering. I looked over to the instructor keeping time and he looked as though he wanted to run off into the woods and scream in laughter.

After the obstacle course was completed, it was time to review our sworn statements with the instructors, who were mostly police investigators. They called me by my number, which made me feel like I was going to be locked up. I sat in front of one of the staff members reading my file. Minimal words were spoken, and then he noticed a hit on my application: child support. I had a significant arrears balance, which I had been paying due to a court order. However, the instructor stated that any new hire could not have this blemish on their application. The look in his face told me that I was immediately disqualified. Thanking him for the opportunity, I walked out toward my truck. I shook my head at the thought of the bad luck I was facing, and for a brief moment I seriously contemplated grabbing my gun and blowing my head off. The setting during my afternoon drive back to Hinesville was indicative of my mood: cold, rainy, and lonely.

Arriving in town, I got a bite to eat, and I finally made it home around 5:30 p.m. The house that I was living in was completely empty. In addition, due to lack of money, I was using a beat up beach chair in my living room to sit in. Emotionally spent, I plopped down in that flimsy chair and just stared into oblivion. Now that I think back at that moment, it felt like something higher than me had manipulated the sedated me. Yes, I had just come off a long drive and had just eaten, but the way I shut down felt like a switch had been tripped. Sitting slumped, my mind went blank. However, I was still coherent. Then I heard my inner voice say, "She's looking too!" I didn't move, because I couldn't. Internally, I became aware and saw nothing but white space. Suddenly, a head came through the white space, like someone snorkeling and probing around in shallow water. It was that female entity, and her face was less than six inches away from my nose. She positioned her head in alignment with mine and just stared. Her head was well proportioned, and her eyes were big and a bit slanted. She didn't look like the aliens we see in the movies. The pupil of hers eyes were the most beautiful blue I'd ever witnessed. Like blue crystal, not even the famous Hope Diamond could radiate such majesty! All I could do was sit and stare in awe of her. Then she inched a little closer in order to read my mind, and her mesmerizing diamond blue eyes rapidly scanned. I couldn't move at all. Helpless, I was slightly amused by the smile she had on her face. I just hope she didn't come across anything dirty in there! When she finished scanning, we both remained in the same up-close position.

"What is your name?" I asked her.

"Xza…" she said, inaudibly.

"What? I can't make it out," I exclaimed. She said her name a few more time, yet I couldn't discern the syllables. Then she switches my focus to a writing pad and spells it out for me: Xzabea (pronounced ex-ZAY-bee-ah).

"Oh, okay. Thank you, Xzabea," I responded.

"You are welcome, Chris," she said.

Next, given back control of my body, I woke up. Still sleepy, I didn't want to shower after the drive. However, I wanted to continue my dialog with Xzabea. There were questions I wanted to ask. Lying down on my makeshift bed, it only took me 10 minutes to reconnect during meditation. While I laid flat on my back, Xzabea hovered above me.

My thoughts were fixated on our previous dialog. "Xzabea, can you explain again about engineering the brown-skinned people?"

"We engineered the brown-skinned people that you call Native Americans and the brown people who live in the regions of Mexico, Central America, the Caribbean, and all of South America. Likewise, there are other alien groups who are a part of a massive hybrid project, controlled and headed by me, who engineered the other races on your planet," Xzabea, said.

I asked, "So, you're saying that blacks, whites, and Asians are engineered also by others?"

"Yes," she said calmly.

My mind raced with so many logical questions to ask next, yet I wasn't prepared with any to ask. In addition, I had a sense that she wasn't going to offer this information so easily. She wanted me to think and figure out the clues. "Hmm, that's interesting. How did you engineer us?"

"We engineered mankind with alien DNA and the DNA of the primates on your plane t."

"Primates!" I yelled. "Are you saying that we're made of chimpanzees and gorillas?" I asked sarcastically.

Xzabea could tell that I didn't know much about primates, and she told me to look up definition of the word. To my ignorance and lack of exposure to the field of taxonomy, I hadn't realized that there are hundreds of primates on this planet, and they are categorized into dozens of family groups. After a bit of reflection, it was fascinating and amusing to learn that mankind is an alien-primate hybrid. "Does anyone else on our planet know about this hybrid project?" I asked.

"Yes, many people on your planet know of this; however, they're in more secular communities, such as metaphysics, government, and private sectors. However, the mass populous doesn't know this," Xzabea said.

I listened to her in disbelief. "We can control mankind anytime we want, yet we don't interfere with free will. However, we do monitor humanity's progress, and gender and race don't matter; if we notice that any human is becoming a disease to themselves or the community and doesn't self- correct, then we will terminate them." Xzabea illustrated this by showing me an image of a brown-skinned male they'd engineered with a button on top of his head.

I was having a problem concentrating during the contact, because

I kept trying to wake up. So, in an effort to realign myself with her and like a camera switching lenses, I zoomed in a little too close and saw her full body while lying on her right side.

"Please don't look at my body," Xzabea said politely.

"I'm sorry. I didn't mean to do that," I said respectfully. I think she was amused by our developing relationship.

March 26, 2010

It had been a week or so since our last contact. Around 12:30 a.m., I'm awakened by a presence – it's Xzabea! Now, I could not see her, but I felt her presence inside my head. "Hi Xzabea. Thanks for coming!" I rubbed my eyes to get focused.

"Hello," she responded.

"Xzabea, where are you from?" I asked.

"I'm from the left gallery. Left of what you identify the constellation Lyra," Xzabea said.

As soon as she finished her sentence (and since she likes to leave me clues to work for the answers), she showed me a white landscape and with a large, red, circular object. I excused myself from our dialog and turned on my laptop to find it. I Googled the question, *"What is the constellation left of Lyra?"* My research results were astonishing! The gallery of the constellation left of Lyra has a large red gas formation! This is the red circle formation she had showed me. This constellation is identified as Cygnus, which has one of the brightest stars in the night sky, known as Deneb. Then I studied further, trying to get a closer look at Constellation Cygnus. "Wow!" I said. The red fiery substance through this constellation is Nebula, which is composed of clouds of dust, hydrogen, and other gases. I'm no scientist, but certainly, I had found the constellation left of Lyra!

Sitting in that torn beach chair, it only took me 10 minutes to re-connect. "Xzabea, I found it," I exclaimed excitedly, "and how cool, your description was completely clear!"

"Yes, that is the location."

"Can I ask more of you?" I asked.

"Yes," replied Xzabea.

"I'm not fluent in science lingo, but what planet are you from within the constellation Cygnus?" I asked.

"I'm from Layone. I am royalty and a leader to all on my planet," she said.

Xzabea then showed me an image of a beautiful white skirt, suggesting that it was made of the finest materials not known to mankind (it looked finer than silk). Embedded within this skirt were multiple large sapphire diamonds lit brilliantly! "Whoa!" I voiced loudly. "Xzabea, what are the beings called from Layone?"

"Layonians," she replied.

"What do they look like?" I dared to ask.

"There are two classes: the Physical and the Intellectual. Those of the Physical class are the workers, builders, and the military. This class is considered the subgroup, but they are intelligent and physically strong. However, their flaw is that they can be mischievous and corrupt. The physical presence of this class can be quite intimidating-black in color - they have long and angular shaped heads. Also, their hands are large, with three claw-like extensions – very adaptable. It's this Layonian physical class, existing since the rise of Earth's civilized societies, that has assisted governments and institutions with technologies and guidance on how to control and sustain power over the people in exchange for power and control for themselves." In one motion, she shows me a split image of a Layonian military leader next to an image of a slender Caucasian male. This white male holds a very important office in U.S. government, with royal red carpeting and the American flag on both sides of him. "Your next president will not be what he appears. He will possess all the qualities to charm the masses; he will be in his late 40s to early 50s, tall, handsome, smart, and athletic. Yet, what no one will discover is that your president's body is actually a shell over what lies underneath. It will be the top Layonian military leader who is not playing within the rules of the hybrid project, and he will have infiltrated or what we call a physical meshing with your next president of the United States,"

Xzabea warns. "Within our project rules, aliens are allowed to conscious mesh, and this is what you and I've been doing throughout this dialog. However, physical meshing is not allowed – it violates the laws of life and free will."

Stunned to hear this, I asked, "What is the president's name?"

Xzabea showed me a list of five names; however, I could barely see, as the list was too far away from my line of sight. Yet, I could tell there was one name circled, and it looked like a very simple American name. Like a photo lens trying to focus on its object, my eyes strained to see the names Dan and John or Jon, overlapping each other. Unable to discern the name of this athletic man with the demeanor of someone who grew up in small-town America; I approached the question from another angle. "Tell me this, what presidential ranking order will he be; 45th, 46th, 47th, 48th, or 49th?"

Xzabea showed me four dark grey squares, the first square having a life energy taking form, while the others remained still. Then I knew she was telling me that the successor to President Obama, the 45th President of the United States, will not be who or what he appears to be.

Note: a week after this conversation took place, I contemplated this particular dialog. I wanted to take a closer look at this upcoming president and the treachery within. I viewed an obscure hotel room with cheap white blinds. To my left, I can see the president to be and sitting across from him was someone shrouded in great secrecy. I could feel that the man behind the blackened out energy represented some old and powerful institution. This further confirmed what Xzabea had told me earlier that there are secret institutions that have collaborated under the direction of this alien military leader and others since the beginning of time. In exchange for wealth and power, they are to help this wayward alien get what he wants – more power over mankind. However, when I panned back to the man that one day will be president, immediately I knew he was different. He's currently 45-47 years old with dark hair and is very handsome. But his eyes were a dead giveaway; his pupils radiated a strange bluish grey color that revealed that he's not of this world. The next vision I saw was his dog,

a Chihuahua on a distinctive leash. The dog will be the First Dog and a
strong selling point with the Hispanic population.

Xzabea then described the other Layonian class of Beings. "The other Layonians are the Intellectual class and are the rulers of the Physical class. Members of this class are highly advanced and work in the fields of engineering and science; they are ultra-intelligent. This class also provides mankind with information to advance. However, there may be conflict between the intellectual class and some rogue hierarchies of the physical class on matters of information dissemination." She paused so I could keep up. "The physical bodies of the Intellectual class are substantially weaker than the sub-group. They appear enfeebled, with a white to light grey tone. However, this group is inherently dominant. Also, members of this superior class have facial features that slightly resemble those of humans, and even their skin texture is similar to your kind. The eyes are slightly larger than yours, yet a major identifying feature of our intellectual group is that their eye colors range from deep blue to bluish grey," she explained. "However, I'm of a royal hierarchy whose eyes display the pure sapphire coloration, with streams of platinum light."

Next she showed me a larger image of the star Deneb in reference to her planet, Layone. Then, like a telescope zooming in, she showed me her planet and its core. The planet looked barren and lifeless. "What happened?" I asked.

"It has been depleted of its resources," she said sadly.

"Where does your race live, now?"

Her answer to my question blew my mind. "We live in the trees, here on your planet!" Xzabea said.

I must have looked confused, because she paused, and then clarified, "Chris, we live *in* the trees."

"How is that possible?" I asked skeptically.

"What the vast majority of you don't know, including your scientists and leaders, is that your trees are portals to another dimension. You just can't see it. We've been right in front of man since the beginning of time."

As I listened intently, Xzabea showed me the center of a tree from her perspective. The environment and energy I saw looked like the pristine, pure turquoise water at Punta Cana, Dominican Republic! The turquoise substance sustains life. As she showed me this, Xzabea continued to speak. "Those of us from Layone, of which I am royalty, live in the trees. We prefer very old and large ones, and we like trees with moss and massive trunks. However, we can communicate and travel and monitor through any type of tree, plant, or vegetation." Next she showed me a map of both North America and South America through a vision, and explained. "Every place *below* this red line is where we live, within the trees." She said.

> Note: the red line started up near the coast of Washington state and ran midway through Oregon, including ¾ of Nevada, ½ of Utah, ½ of Colorado, a small section of Kansas, ¾ of Oklahoma, most of Arkansas, all of Mississippi, and all of the southeastern states. The red boundary also included all of Mexico, Central America, the Caribbean, and South America.

When Xzabea finished explaining this to me, she instructed me that, when I awoke, I was to go to Savannah, Georgia! Our communication ended at 4:30 a.m. Exhausted, I slept until 10:00 a.m. Once fully awake, I compiled all of my notes and paused at the instruction to go to Savannah. *Why Savannah?* I asked myself. I've been there once but knew nothing about it.

Savannah is about 30 miles from Hinesville. There are many routes to get there. The route I took was from US 84 to US 17 straight into the city limits of Savannah. I didn't know what to look for; she had just told me to go. Truth be told, the drive and scenery were boring. I'm not much for small towns and vast country – it kind of gives me the creeps. US 17 led me to a split within the city limits. I had to make a decision to take 80 west or east. So, I followed a hunch to travel east. About 10 minutes into the drive, I saw some massive and majestic trees! I said, "Holy __." Along Victory Boulevard, the trees stood firm with their canopies spread wide. I stumbled upon a park named Daffin Park. Entering, but before exploring it, I had to know what type of trees those were. After looking it up on my Blackberry, I learned that they were oak trees with Spanish moss hanging from them. The life span of one of these oaks can be up to 300 years!

I took a stroll through Daffin Park, which had these huge oaks throughout its property. I still wasn't sure why Xzabea told me to come here. Ten minutes later, I had the notion to place my palm flat against the surface of one particular oak tree. As soon as I had done so, I quickly switched my focus toward my solar plexus. A surge of energy shot through my arm! Amazed by the feeling, I reasoned that Xzabea had probably wanted me to come here to feel of the life force that's within these trees.

Over the next 4 or 5 days I followed the same routine. I'd drive to that park in Savannah and enjoy the scenery and experience the force of those massive oaks. Being there helped me better understand how close to Nature we really are.

Occasionally as I walked about, I'd touch one of those old compatriots and got the same tingling and energizing sensation!

One day I drove to Skidaway Island State Park, located near Savannah. The park sits on Skidaway Island, which is part of the Atlantic Intracoastal Waterway. This island houses acres of forest and marshes and all kinds of animals; Skidaway is an ideal place for nature lovers. The park is surrounded by private housing communities, and there were lots available for campers and RVs. There's a $5 fee for a 1-day pass. I drove around for a while on this island, but that was no way to get the full effect; walking is the only mode of travel through this park. I walked up a long, narrow path and greeted others who were also enjoying the sights. In addition, I saw two guys walking about lazily and dreamy eyed, but I doubt they were looking at trees and animals!

Going the opposite direction of Touchy and Feely, I went to an area that seemed exceptionally quiet in comparison to the other sections with foot trails. To get the effect of the natural surroundings, i expanded my awareness and had a strong sense that I was being watched, not only by

Xzabea, but by several others as well. It felt like I was in the presence of eminence!

Near the end of the week, I was bored of visiting Savannah, yet seeing and touching those oaks will be a lasting memory. During the evening, I connected with Xzabea, and she came within minutes. First, I thanked her for sending me there and reported that seeing those oaks was unlike anything I'd seen up north or west. Curious, I asked her about my walk in the Forrest at Skidaway Park, and the feeling that was there some type of eminence watching me. Strangely, I sensed that she was withholding her answer, so I didn't push it. I also mentioned how, while in Daffin Park, each time I placed my palm against a tree, a rush of energy would shoot up my arm. "What was that?" I asked.

She replied, "I was touching you."

CHAPTER 7

EVEN ALIENS HAVE "HATERS"

APRIL 2, 2010. On this night, I just wanted to relax and not connect with anyone. The day had been uneventful, as I had visited the Ft. Stewart employment page to see if any of the eight job postings I had applied for turned up any results. Nothing! All eight applications were denied. Feeling the familiar stress of being rejected, I went up the street and got a 20oz. can of beer to take the edge off. A lightweight as a drinker, I caught a quick buzz and fell asleep early.

In the middle of the night, I felt an unusually strong psychic impression. Above my head and I could sense space opening up, as light was revealed. But something didn't seem right. I went into viewing mode, but couldn't make out the details. There seemed to be some skirmish between Xzabea and someone else; I don't know who. Whoever this larger and darker thing was, he wanted to occupy the space that connected me to Xzabea. This actually felt very dangerous. I immediately interrupted their argument and shoving and said, "I choose Xzabea, not you!" As soon as I said that, this dominant strong arm made a growling sound and took out a blade and slashed Xzabea's throat. When this happened, the bright light above me went dim. I saw Xzabea lying on a floor with a serious gash on her throat and her spine almost severed. All of a sudden, like an angry husband ripping up love letters found from his cheating wife, this creature raised his large black claw with three thick fingers- grabbed all of the visions and messages between me and Xzabea and crushed them. Then he ran off, laughing.

woke up feeling deeply disturbed about what had happened to Xzabea. I tried to contact her, but got no answer. I'm sure she wasn't dead, but her life energy had gone dim. After about 30 minutes of no contact, I went into full viewing capability. I tried to connect with her peers or anyone who could give me answers. I wasn't going to stop until I found her or found out if she was all right. Then I found her! She was lying on a metal table, but I could only see her feet. From her knees up were cloaked in darkness. I didn't know what this meant. Is she alive or dead? Wait! I felt she was alive!

In all my life, I've made some dumb mistakes and missteps. Yet, the one thing in life I am not is a coward. I am not afraid to fight and protect those whom I care about. Since God gave me this extraordinary gift and an understanding of the ways of the spirit, that night my only goal was to heal Xzabea with every vibration that I could pull together.

Using the image of her lying on the table; I started with her feet and created a bluish-white spiral of energy and slowly and methodically worked my way up her body. Eventually, I completely engulfed her with the brightest light I could create. This experience lasted until I was exhausted. No way could I let her down, especially when she'd comforted me during the most tumultuous period of my life! At some point I stopped sending out these healing thoughts toward Xzabea and rested. During those few minutes, I could see entities that looked like doctors operating on her. Her wounds looked severe, but I felt certain that she would come out okay. Weakly, I heard her say mentally, "Thank you for being there for me!"

Before she trailed off, I wanted to know what had attacked her. "What the hell was that thing!?"

She replied, "That was Goneh; he gets jealous of me."

"Who is he?" I asked.

"He's part of the Royal military Force. He's high ranking," she said. Her energy was low, so I didn't want to tire her out. I told her we'd talk again soon and ended the transmission.

Apparently Goneh had an issue with me, as later that morning he kept coming into that space where he could touch me consciously. I felt his presence. He kept taunting me and trying to get my attention, but instead of being afraid, I kept balanced and centered on the power of my subconscious mind. I kept one single idea: that I was protected in the name of Jesus Christ. I think this pissed him off.

Because I had the white light of Christ surrounding me, Goneh he literally stuck his hand within the ray of conscious energy radiating from my head to demonstrate his great power. However, I kept steady and did not give ground. In a final act of defiance, he flipped a cigar butt from his realm into my psyche. Like a still pond being disturbed by a rock, I could not get his name out of my mind. The vibration of waves created by that cigar butt permeated my thoughts like an addiction for three days. It was like my wires had gotten crossed. Admittedly, I was getting concerned, because it felt like I had a nervous tic from my constantly thinking about and wanting to say his name. The only thing for me to do was keep calling on the cleansing and protective power of Jesus Christ. On the third day, the disturbance finally went away, and I told myself, "Hell no, I ain't never messing around with that guy!"

Realizing that he could not disturb me, Goneh left me alone and went down toward Brazil to manipulate, corrupt, and tempt vulnerable men and boys into licentious behavior. Thrown into same-sex addictions, they had no clue as to what lies beneath and is manipulating them to do such acts.

A few days later, I checked on Xzabea, and apparently Goneh had had her removed to a secluded and heavily forested area in the northwestern part of Brazil. One of her peers told me that she had to be moved, because she's High Royalty; she's not supposed to get to close to me and others in order to allow her to heal from her attack. One time, while I was viewing her, she was sitting in front of a vanity mirror, crying. Sensing that I was viewing her, Xzabea turned around, and to my surprise she was growing out blonde hair! It was a striking picture along with her diamond blue eyes. Strangely, over the next several days I would dream of Xzabea as a blonde, or I would see a blonde and blue eyed woman around me in visions. One morning, I awoke to a platinum blonde woman with blue eyes and a seductive smile, hovering over and staring at me! I asked quietly, "What are you up to, Xzabea? "

Since her violent incident, Xzabea communicated at a safe distant and was careful not to cross over that threshold that allows her to be within my conscious and physical realm. Confusingly, when she'd speak to me, I kept seeing some blonde haired woman at a distance and walking towards me. In a recent vision there was a blonde woman lying on the ground of that park I used to visit in Savannah. Rising off the ground from a sleeping position, her body was made up of tree leaves that presented the definition of feminine curves and form. Her hair was flowing beautifully and bright, as she took off at a run. *Running where?* I wondered.

Later in the day, I turned on the TV, and the major news networks were captivated by a terrible tragedy that had hit the Gulf of Mexico. An offshore oil rig owned by one of the largest oil companies in the world had exploded, killed several people, and caused a massive oil spill. All of the coastal states that access the Gulf had been affected adversely. Wildlife had been poisoned and was dying off in growing numbers, and the local economies that thrive off the coastal business had come to a halt. This disaster made me both sad and angry.

That evening, I went to bed early, still mentally exhausted from the psychological and spiritual fight with Goneh. Therefore, to help ease my mind, I sought to engage in light meditation, just enough to lull me to sleep. Before I slipped into unconsciousness, I saw deep on the ocean floor, large and skinny spider-like hands pulling up some earth encrusted hatch that was 3' feet beneath the surface. The black hands with yellow strips along the middle fingers were extremely long and clearly not native to our planet. With the hatch fully opened, I saw the top of an apparatus or chamber. Fully conscious within, I switched my attention back over to Xzabea, because I wanted to know what I was about to see. Though she was at a faraway hiding place, I could still connect mentally.

"Xzabea, I hope you're feeling better. I recently received a vision of the deep ocean. There were some very large hands pulling up some hatch. It looked like some safe box or a capsule... I had a hard time figuring it out. What is this?" I asked.

"Uh huh, I see it; however, Chris, I'm too weak to explain this to you now. I want you to go back to it and see for yourself," she replied.

"Okay, I understand. Please heal yourself, and we'll talk later," I said. I hadn't realized that she was in so much pain.

I woke up so I could re-approach the underwater vision with a fresh mind. Logically, I started thinking about the horrendous oil spill out on the Gulf. Then I asked myself the question of whether there was any correlation between my vision and this oil spill. I stepped outside to get some fresh air and came back in to meditate. Immediately, I connected with the energy signal that showed me the deep underwater message. I replayed the image and fixed onto the last thing I saw, which was the top of that safe or capsule. Relaxed and focused on the object, I saw it rise slowly out of its chamber. It rose like a powerful missile out of its silo. It was a six- to eight-foot-long capsule, and inside of it was churning water and mud and rocks. I could sense that something was in the center of this stirring and earthy concoction. At this moment, I kept performing checks and balances with myself, to ensure that this was not something that my mind was creating. Yet, upon further analysis, I confirmed that I was seeing this capsule filled with murky water. I stared at it for five minutes until I heard an androgynous voice say, "I do not want to be revealed!" Respecting this entity and remaining cautious, I asked, "Does your presence have anything to do with the current oil spill in the Gulf of Mexico?" There was silence for about three minutes, and no answer was given. I could tell that this thing was being extremely cautious with me because of my talent to pick up the most subtle of energy vibrations, and it wished not to reveal its identity. Determined to learn the reason why I was seeing this, I asked a different question: "Are you here to hurt us, or do you have other intentions?" Yet again, I received no answer from this thing standing in the center of the watery and cloaked chamber.

I hadn't realized that, during my attempt to communicate with this being inside that chamber, Xzabea was watching and listening. "Connect over here, Chris," said Xzabea.

"Yes Xzabea?" I asked.

"Look inside this," she said.

Xzabea opened up what looked like a small flap of the Earth's surface. I saw that turquoise-colored environment that I remember seeing in the center of that tree when Xzabea had explained to me the other dimension of resources and vibrant life within the trees. Inside this healing environment were massive machine gears, but they were not operating.

"What's this? I remember this turquoise environment you shown to me earlier. But what are those gears for?" I asked, confused.

"The entity that doesn't want to be revealed – a wish you should honor – is here to help your nation clean up this unnecessary oil spill and restore your ocean and its wildlife back to health. Chris, it is important to know, without its help, your nation will be unable to repair the damage," Xzabea explained. As soon as Xzabea told me this, she further showed me a white backdrop. In the center were large black hands wringing out a sponge of oil and sludge. She told me that, on August 6, 2010, an alien entity that had been placed in the deepest part of our ocean would rise in the Gulf of Mexico to assist us to restore our oceans back to health. Without its help, we would never be able to correct the ecological damage that has been done.

CHAPTER 8

IMMINENCE AND EMINENCE

O N April 30, my truck got repossessed. That was it! That was the final straw! There were no words to describe how I felt. At this point I had no wheels, living in a country town that had no bus system. I hadn't walked anywhere since I was 18 years old! How embarrassing. I was now immobilized and limited to the stores within 2 or 3 blocks from me. My ego wasn't that big, but I hated to walk to and from places to eat or to do laundry. Folks looked at me like I was some reject; I did not like that at all.

One day, I was walking home from a local hole-in-the-wall of a restaurant (but it had great chicken wings!). Tired from the humidity, I decided to take a nap. Within 20 minutes of resting and without trying, I saw myself entering some large, open hall. Standing around me were members of the Layonian military. Big and black mean-looking dudes, their bodies looked like armor. They all stood there, just staring at me, when suddenly they cleared the way for their military leader. When I caught sight of him, I realized – it was Goneh! He's the thing that kept instigating me. I started reciting the Lord's Prayer, and fast. Like the cowardly lion from the Wizard of Oz, I was about to "break camp!" He was their top military leader. Goneh looked super strong and bad ass, with some black and obscure-looking crown that had a *live* rotating sun in its center! Interestingly, I could see Xzabea standing in the shadows to the right side of his throne.

This superior military leader was equally confused and a bit shocked when he saw me. He jumped up from his throne and stepped to the lower floor to get a better look at me. When he stepped from his throne, those inferior to him got out of his way immediately. Goneh stood about 10 feet from me and gawked in disbelief. It was like he was saying, this *scrawny looking brotha – again?* Personally, I didn't know what was happening. Therefore, just like those inferior soldiers, I got the hell out the way and disappeared.

When I brought myself back to reality and tried to sleep, I was brought back to Goneh. I was at the same location as before. I was looking about his military force, and all eyes were on Goneh. Now I stood before him in disbelief! He was talking on a cellular device, listening with his right ear. There was much chatter from the soldiers, and then Goneh threw his arm up, motioning for them to shut up. While he was listening, behind him, a massive sphere of bright light emerged. The enormity of this thing was beyond comprehension. I was getting unnerved, and I looked to see if Xzabea was still there (she wasn't – I think she hauled ass!). Everyone was standing there, transfixed at the presence of the orb; even Goneh's demeanor had lowered a couple of notches. Then everyone looked to the right of this majestic and massive energy. Some translucent entity approached and observed me from a higher elevation. Whatever this was, it was definitely Eminence, but of what? The body appearance, though you could see through it, was almost like Xzabea's structure. This strange entity stared and looked right through me. In my lifetime, I had never seen anything like this. The fear that went up my spine was unexplainable. Piercing black eyes with no hair and no discernable facial features, this supreme entity held a round black bag with two interlocking zippers. It then turned the bag to reveal the teeth of the zippers for me to see. "Look!" she said, and vanished.

Physically shaking, I woke up immediately. The presence of that being had me scared so badly that I was beginning to cower. Writing notes in my journal, I pondered, "Who the hell was he?" Then a voice from nowhere interjected: *She!*

Breaking Point

May 4, 2010. My life hadn't gotten any better. In fact, I don't know where or what I was doing anymore. My job search was a joke. The situation for me has been made worst with the repossession of my truck. Broken and beaten down, the only thing that kept me sane was the contact with the alien; how ironic. But what good were these strange experiences doing me? The truth was that my life was truly screwed up, and I was tired of feeling like a loser. At this point, I'd fallen into a severe depression. There was nothing I could do or anyone to talk to. My friends would never understand what I had seen; they couldn't understand. All they could offer is half-hearted sympathy like, "You'll be all right." No, they could never understand.

When I woke up that morning, the pain in my heart for my damaged life was unbearable. I was exhausted with prayer and didn't want to face another day of disappointment. Like a heavy bag of bricks, this nagging sensation in my gut had to be let go, and as if something took control of my hand, I picked up my pen and wrote this letter – a suicide letter:

2:30 p.m. *"God, I don't want to do this anymore. I'm worn out from trying to figure it out and don't understand why this has to be so hard. All of my life, I've walked the path as you taught us. My life has never been disrupted with violence or recklessness. I've taken care of my body and mind and lived in moderation. Tell me how a man can do his best to balance relationships, money, and self; not be met with the same blessing and love that life has to offer? Even in mathematics, if the correct numbers are entered into an equation, then the end result is balanced and correct. I know men from all walks of life who are inherently corrupt and fowl, yet they walk on this earth with fat pockets and feed their faces with gluttony and flesh. I know women who are the filthiest specimens to even harbor DNA who adorn themselves with jewels and perfumes to hide their piercing stench. These people walk around having jobs, cars, and money abundant in their lives. I don't get it. Fifteen years, and without anyone ever knowing, I've given thousands of dollars away in secret to the homeless, both black and white, who didn't know I was coming. I have* *also known people who will pimp their own 7-year-old daughters on the streets so that they can continue to support their addiction to crack. March 6, 1993 was the beginning of the longest walk of my life. I searched, inquired, and sacrificed the good will of my family and friends to protect something within, which I don't understand. God, I'm done. I can't do it. I don't want to do it. I now call on you to end my life – now!"*

I had snapped! With each syllable written and thoughts formed, anger was building up inside me that had a mind of its own. After the pen lifted, I went to the back room and opened a black luggage case and pulled out my .22 caliber pistol that I had held in secrecy. For the previous five years I had always carried that pistol but never brandished it or talked about it. It was only meant for an absolute last measure of defense. In that moment, I had become something darker while sitting in that taped up beach chair and trying to recite the Lord's prayer. Then I heard a voice say, "You must kill yourself" and then my body went numb. Feeling strangely disoriented, the gun in my hand felt very heavy. That voice said again, "You must kill yourself." Slumped over, the room started spinning- it's like I've been drugged. Again, the voice presses me to kill myself and i hypnotically snatched back the charging handle, placed the muzzle firmly against my right temple, and pulled the trigger!

The deathly sound of that metal click and the thump of the gun jumping out my hand and hitting the wall brought me back to reality. My heart was beating so hard it felt like it was banging against the back of my chest. Slumped over, my eyes were blurred with tears and drool and gargling noises were coming out of my mouth. I was trying to determine if I was dead or alive. Strangely, there was the smell of cheap paint and the odor of insecticide from a recent spraying. Upon smelling these common household scents, I realized that I was still alive. The gun must have misfired. However, I couldn't reason or think; it was like I was in a coma. Like the unpleasant sensation when someone throws cold water in your face, something had put me in a trance. It was Xzabea, and I heard her say, "Remember when I said that we engineered man?" When she asked that, I saw myself sitting on a stool against the backdrop of wheat fields waving freely. I sat on the stool, sedated, and one of Xzabea's scientist peers reached over and opened up my forehead. He pulled it down like a dirty ashtray in a car. From my vision, I could see what was going on; inside my head and around the frontal lobe was pitch blackness. Then the scientist took a syringe filled with a bright blue fluid and injected it into my frontal lobe and the surrounding areas. The vision ended. I faded to sleep.

CHAPTER 9

WHAT RELIGION HAS TRIED TO HIDE

WHEN I awakened, I was surprised to see that I was still alive. However, physically, I felt like I had been beaten up. After freshening up, I decided to take a walk and get something to eat. This time, walking around exposed didn't bother me. My ego wasn't affected by the loss and humiliation as a 45-year-old man who once had a great lifestyle filled with women, a beautiful home, and the latest-model Mercedes, Hummer, and BMW.

I decided on Chinese food, even though I'm a bit shy when it comes to this type of menu. The food at this place was clean and tasty. My favorite was a dish called Singapore Noodles, which had yellow curry spice and was packed with chicken, shrimp and pork. While waiting for the meal to be prepared, I gazed out the restaurant window and out across the parking lot. An acre of land across the way featured towering oaks with their canopies spreading wide. They were beautiful specimens with branches so large that you could hang three 20-ton bright red and chromed fire trucks on them like ornaments on a Christmas tree. I stared at them and had the sensation that Xzabea was in one of those trees, beckoning to me. Acknowledging her, I finished my meal and headed home. I walked through the greenbelt with those oaks. While walking passed them, I deliberately slowed my pace and glided my right hand across one of the trunks. I felt the same tingling sensation that I had felt at that park in Savannah. That was my confirmation that Xzabea wanted my attention. I quickened my pace.

Admittedly, after having eaten, my energy was too high to meditate. Therefore, I played some healing instrumental music on my Blackberry playlist that always put me in a calmer mood. Forty-five minutes later, I eventually became sedated enough to make contact. Then I had clear vision, clearer than it had ever been! "There's that enormous energy sphere again," I said to myself. It was so brilliant, yet not blinding. I could sense that the depth and the complexity of this presence would be immeasurable by man. Nothing in man's arsenal of technology could contain it. This phenomenon was beyond words. Xzabea walked out of a perfect white field with a tall figure. Xzabea was smiling, and her sapphire eyes were gleaming as bright as the globe behind her. "Hi, Chris. I brought him here to fix your life!"

I stared in disbelief while she held the hand of this entity. With Xzabea vanishing out of the picture, it was just this entity and me standing before each other. He walked closer, and I can see him more clearly. My eyeballs damned near popped out! He approached me wearing a long white robe that draped to his ankles. I looked down at his feet and noticed he wore dark brown sandals. His left hand was reached out to me, and I noticed how earthy and strong it looked. Even the veins of his hand looked like robust grape vines. I looked at his face and saw that his cheek area was pitted and rough, yet he was handsome. His eyes were deep set and dark, but more strangely, a mysterious cloud with immeasurable depth shaded his eyes. However, what confused me was his head piece. It was a keffiyeh! He walked slowly toward me; then something began to emanate from him. The first name that came to my mind was *Messiah*, but this word didn't seem to fit. He could tell that my mind was struggling to keep up. To me, spiritually, metaphysically, and mentally, nothing added up! It felt like I was going to pass out from the overwhelming emotion.

The tall, mysterious figure spoke. "I'm here to help my people." I said nothing but continued to just stare at him.

He repeated himself. "I'm here to help my people, and you're going to help me."

This didn't make sense to me, since I couldn't even fix my own life, let alone help a whole people. "How am I to help you?"

"You are to deliver our message."

My focus is clear, but I was kind of scared to continue. "What message is that?" I asked.

He said in a commanding voice, "You," and I instinctively understood that he meant mankind collectively, "cannot rise any higher than your current position."

I was stunned; he had spoken the exact words my mother had said to me when I was 15 years old. My mom wasn't exactly the type to sit her children down and explain the facts of life. Her method was a bit more aloof. As she did her daily routine throughout the house, Mom would ramble on about a life subject. Therefore, the onus was on us kids to catch her wisdom in passing. One day and while sitting on the living room stairs, mom looked over to me and said, "Remember, Chris, you cannot rise any higher than your current position." All of my adult life, her statement served as a riddle for me. I couldn't decipher as to what it meant. So, when I heard this male entity say the exact same thing, now he had my attention. "Will you explain that, please?"

"Yes," he said. "Mankind cannot rise any higher that his current position. Nearing the end of the year 2012, his evolution will be stopped. The only way man can continue to grow is to be open and receptive to new ideas and truths about him and about me."

"Who are you?" I asked.

My conversation with this tall figure was interrupted by that very powerful entity that I saw earlier in the military chamber. I then remembered the voice that told me that *He* was a *She*! I became nervous and tense. She peered through me like I wasn't there. Her eyes were more dark and intense than a snake. This female presence frightened me to no end! "What is your name?" I asked sheepishly.

"That cannot be revealed until you look!" she replied.

Once again, she held a black, round bag with two interlocking zippers on it. I didn't understand; why was she telling me to look? The item was cloaked tightly, and I was becoming flustered. Determined, the female figure placed the black round bag with the zippers directly in front of my face and forcibly told me to look. With an investigative eye, I peered between the zippers of that bag and gasped. "Oh my God, that's Earth! There's been a great design and a dark concealment of your identity from everyone who has ever walked and now walks on this planet. There have been oaths, blood pacts, and allegiances from religious institutions and arrogant men of power to deny you of what is rightfully yours. It has been decided never to speak your name or acknowledge your existence!" I pulled my eyes away from the locked and cloaked object. "Who are you?" I shockingly demanded.

Standing side by side, the male figure and the female figure looked at me with a sense of gratification as though I had cracked some ancient code and said, "We are God!"

"What!" I yelled. It was as if every brick within my psyche had begun to crumble with the light peering through.

The male entity spoke. "The first truth that has to be revealed to all is that God has never been just male, yet God is male/female. Our true names are Hhere/Ccerdi."

I couldn't make out the enunciation, so they wrote it out for me. Hhere (huh-HEE-ree), which is the male aspect, and Ccerdi (seh-SER-dee) is the female aspect.

"How can you have a name, please help me understand?" I asked, confused.

"God is known by many names: King of Kings, Adonai, Brahman, and many others. It doesn't matter to what name is given, and it is according to each faith and path to find and know me; their viewpoint of me is correct. However, no one on your planet has uttered the true name of God, Hhere/Ccerdi, until you. This is our true name. We are one and the same and cannot be separated." Hhere exclaims. "Hhere/Ccerdi are inseparable and are one. We are the creator of the universe and all of life in it. Nothing comes before us, and nothing comes after us. We are all that IS."

Still confused, I felt the need to challenge this. "We never… I mean… I never read or have been told that God is male and female. It's always been assumed that God is masculine."

The intense female entity that wanted me to crack the ancient code of that black bag – Ccerdi, interjects. "Yes, at the beginning of the rise of your civilization, the early intellectuals and priests and priestesses knew of God's true aspect and name. However, as time moved on, they became fearful of me. They could not understand or control the reach of my expansive spirit and deep intuition. Consequently, since they could not control me, they chose to ignore the truth of my existence. These early architects of control and deceit came together and created a pact to erase the female aspect of God and to never speak my name. Thus, if they never speak the name Ccerdi, then it would be natural for them not to speak the name of my counterpart." Ccerdi expressed. "Sadly, the faithful who chose not to follow this great lie were identified as heretic or rivals to the establishment. Unfortunately, these brave men and women were quickly censored or executed at the command of both political and religious leaders of the time. Furthermore, any book or doctrines with my mention were forever destroyed. However, the lies and deception of mankind are short lived and have no weight against truth, and the truth is that we, Hhere/Ccerdi, are God!" Shifting her position in front of me, Ccerdi continued to speak. "This is the reason why mankind attached himself to the masculinity of God and forewent to truly understand his spirituality. Materialism became mankind's half God. This he could control, see, touch, and manipulate."

While I stood in utter disbelief of what I heard, both the male and female God aspects merged into a single and blinding synergy. In a single harmonious voice, God spoke. "We are impressed to the degree that mankind has thrown himself into materialism, but the problem for him now is that his growth has been stopped. There isn't any further evolution to be had materially. The only way mankind can continue to write new chapters in his future is if he, in equal passion, intrepidity, and sacrifice, embraces spirituality."

With respect, I interjected. "God, I don't understand what growing

spiritually really means. I keep hearing this, but no one seems to understand what it actually means. At the turn of the millennium, the entire
world had a new sense of things, yet we lacked clarity about what we
were feeling. Then our new spirituality began to take form in fad called
the Law of Attraction, but that died off within a few years. My mom
was a hippy child of the '60s who had affection for metaphysics, and
all she ever preached was that we must grow spiritually. Yet I couldn't
understand her talk of spiritual stuff. Also, we have preachers, teachers,
religion, and doctrines. Given our current tools and reference, how do
we become more spiritual beyond what we have?" I asked, confused.

"Now you're thinking," God said happily. "The real challenge isn't
that man should grow spiritually; it's needed of him to grow consciously.
Raise your consciousness, and then your spirit will follow. Yet humanity
is dealing with a fundamental problem. Despite his fortitude to survive,
the progression of every man, woman, and child on your planet has been
stopped. The only way that your race can continue to evolve is through
assistance."

Mentally struggling to process this heavy information, I said, "What
do you mean *assisted?*"

"During the rise and building of your civilization and at each stage
of development that marked great advancement, mankind had been
assisted by alien intelligence. In science, medicine, technology, art,
music, and even social activism, your race had been assisted. This is the
only way your race could move forward."

While I listened to this, I felt serious doubt about the entire validity
of all of this conversation and meeting. Skepticism crept into my voice.
"I have doubt about what you're saying. Okay, let's assume that I believe
what you're telling me about aliens assisting us. But, why do we need
help? We are an intelligent race and have done okay up to this point."

God retorts. "It's not a matter of intelligence, but it's more about
what's happened to the spirituality of humanity. All of you are too far
removed from what's true, and you lack an understanding of what's
needed to correctly evolve your species. Therefore, it's imperative that
your world embrace the alien life that is waiting and wanting to help

your world advance. Their involvement in your lives is highly crucial, but the primary reason as to why alien life awaits to connect with you is to protect you."

"Protect us from what?" I asked.

"Satan!" God says in a lower decibel. Hhere/Ccerdi stepped out of their synergy and concluded our meeting that night. They assured me that the dialog would continue, and they motioned me to sleep.

When I woke up, I felt drunk, and my skin felt cold and clammy. I looked at the time on my phone and noticed that I couldn't account for two hours that had passed. I walked outside to get fresh air and to gather my thoughts. A few hours earlier, I had tried to kill myself. Yet, I thought, *I think that alien girl interfered with the gun misfiring, and she introduced me to God. Did they tell me their names were Hhere/Ccerdi? What was all that talk about aliens helping mankind advance in life?* Many questions raced through my mind, and I was as confused as I had been when I started.

CHAPTER 10

MATTER OF PERCEPTION

May 5, 2:47 a.m.

IN an instant, I realized that I was standing in some perfectly white space with flashes of gold light around me. Mesmerized, I noticed within feet of me Hhere kneeling and working on what looked like a large car engine. This didn't make sense to see God working on this engine in this magical looking place, especially if he really was God. Staring at him tinkering with that block of metal, I chose to ignore my curiosity and address something more pressing on my mind.

"Hello, Hhere!" I greeted.

"Hello Chris!" responded God, as he continued working on that engine.

I didn't see Ccerdi, but I could tell she was close. "Hhere, earlier I met an alien named Xzabea. She told me that they (Layonians) created the Brown people on earth."

"That's correct," said Hhere.

"She also said that there are other and multiple alien intelligences that are involved in some hybrid project on earth, and they engineered the other races of people. Is this correct?"

He got up slowly and moved towards me. "Yes," said Hhere, in a calm voice.

"But, how's this possible, aren't you God?!" I asked.

Hhere stopped and looked down at me. "I, Hhere/Ccerdi, am the creator of the universe and everything in it and all of you are our children. Just as we give you the power of free will, likewise, we give alien life the same power of free will to choose and create and experience what they desire. The multiple alien species within the region of your space decided to come together in one design and with the goal to create mankind. This newly engineered species was to become a path of salvation for the aliens. The alien/primate project on your planet has multiple objectives, but one focus of the project is for aliens to experience through mankind an experience that is the opposite of what they are. Similar to each of your having certain inadequacies in life, there are many aliens who have their own pains and desires. As an example, some aliens wanted to experience through man what laughter is like or how it feels to make love. Others wanted to experience crying and some to suffer extreme hunger. Interestingly, there was a group of aliens who were curious enough to be enslaved in shackles and their neighbors from other planets wanted to oblige them by becoming heartless oppressors. Whatever their desire – pain, want, or angst – aliens were brilliant enough to bring mankind to life and experience liberation through each of you." Hhere could tell that I was having a difficult time keeping up mentally, and he paused a moment. "The key to the aliens' experience beyond themselves depends on crucial elements that had to exist. When we, Hhere/Ccerdi, created Earth, we placed it in a specific part of the universe. In reference to the universe, the very spot where Earth spins has a dense vibration. This is important, because this spin and density give rise to an intuitive female energy. This expansive energy is extremely powerful and has been built within Earth's physical structure and moves so slow and peculiar that it can break up, permeate, and/or transcend any form of matter. Just like water washing over rocks, there's an immediate dynamic movement that is refreshing and gives rise to new smells, feelings, and visuals. Another important element for alien experience is your planet's natural host. Primates are the true inheritors of your world, and they harness in their DNA this expansive female energy that's instinctive, intuitive, and emotional. The next important element is the gravitational pull from the celestial bodies that make up your solar system. Each varying movement weighs on your planet and slows it down to degrees of vibration that become sublime." Hhere smiled at me. "When you add life (primates) and alien intelligence, to whom are powered by intention upon a playing field that is just as live and electrifying, the end result is fascinating experiences."

Now, while I was listening to Hhere, part of my vision could see some Layonians behind controls similar to that of an operations center. I could also tell that they were operating from some strange dimension. These were of the Intellect class. Their facial features looked almost human, yet it was easily discernable that there was something very different about them. This operations group each wore a blue top with a red garment pulled over their shoulders. I could tell that they were amused with my dialog with God.

Hhere then walked over to a hovering 36" vertical band of black and white murky energy. I'm curious to what he's studying. "What's that?" I asked.

"Life on Earth; I'm monitoring man," said Hhere.

"How are you monitoring them? I don't see anything recognizable as people – it looks like a murky cloud," I said.

Looking at me patiently, HHERE replied, "What you're seeing is the life force of all of mankind. The agitation and meshing of white, black, and grey energy are actually souls moving in and out of multiple levels of conscious dimensions."

"Hmm, I don't understand. Why are our souls in that vertical state and not spread out or in a bunched-up position?" I asked.

"Later I'll go into detail as to what you're looking at, but for now I'll give you a brief explanation. Outside of your perception, logic, and physical world, energy, ideas, and objects take on a different form and movement relative to their speed, time, and position. Your scientists and spiritual teachers have gone to great lengths to explain space and time; they call it the space-time continuum. They're also correct in their explanation of the relationship of space being three dimensional and time being one dimensional. Combining these two dimensions makes a single construct, like a map of an area representing a union of things. This area and union of all things lays the foundation that becomes important in the dialog about spatial and temporal space. Attention to spatial and temporal space reveals that time is not what you think it is. Space-time is relativistic to any given object, and this theory suggests that it's not time that moves, but it the object itself that is moving," Hhere said patiently. "In addition, your spiritual teachers understand that this space/time dialog about your outer world can also be reduced to non-physical properties within the inner world – the spiritual. Within the spiritual realm, the fabric or area that connects all things is the soul, and the non-physical object that moves about the soul is consciousness. It's important to know that, when I speak about the fabric of the soul, I'm not speaking in individual terms, but something much larger and complex that I'll explain later," Hhere said assuredly. "But, for this conversation, it's important for you to understand why this space/time conversation relates to you personally and to your question of why those souls are in a vertical position and not spread out. Starting with events set in motion beyond your control, you personally were put on a course to be stripped of every material object, person, and activity that preoccupied your mind. Now, all of these things and people and objects are not separate from you and are occupying the same fabric or space that you're occupying and either moving or not moving at the same rate of speed relative to your position and awareness. With your current temporal rhythm, you're prone only to see, attract, and connect with things that are moving and vibrating at your awareness within the fabric, which is complex with material and spiritual matter. Changes in your life and removal of any preoccupying factor forced you into a position of total isolation and concentration on yourself. After all, you had no choice in this matter. Moreover, by relegating you to nothing (so to speak), all of the things that slowed your vibration and blinded your inner vision were removed. The end result allowed your level of awareness to rise to extraordinary levels within the fabric and beyond physical matter that floats and coagulates together. Rising over all matter within the fabric of your world doesn't mean you've separated yourself from old relationships and ideas, for they still exist and are moving in the same direction as you, but you've repositioned yourself from them. This repositioning actually means that your consciousness has sped up and connected to another reference point within the fabric. Therefore, both science and spiritualism suggest that, if an object can manipulate time by moving to various positions within the fabric, then there is no past, present, or future in the classical sense. In addition, whether it's a conversation about our spatial universe or expansive reach of one's soul, the past, present, and future are not separate reality points, yet reference points independent to each object or thought in motion. Therefore, to answer your question of why it is vertical, it's vertical based on the fact that the past, present, and future are all happening right now. Just as I have given your scientists and philosophers brilliant minds to discover and analyze this phenomenon, I have given you the gift of sight to actually see it. All of it is happening right now!" explained Hhere.

"Forgive me for saying this, but based on that explanation and what I'm looking at, I do not see anything that suggests Heaven and Hell, in the classical sense. All I see is energy moving and shifting and merging in one single up-and-down reality," I said.

"You are correct. All of your lives (past, present, and future) are happening in the vertical now. You are moving in and out of multiple levels of consciousness and experiencing all of you. There is nothing separate from your experience to suggest Heaven and Hell. These two extremes, just like many potential reference points within the space-time continuum, are constructions of the mind. A person moving about their space and depending on their reference frame of mind will choose where they decide to be, so if they choose the worst pain and suffering imaginable, then that's where they will be, and time will slow down. Yet if they choose liberation over fear, they'll experience only jubilation and peace; thus time for them is light and fast. Heaven and Hell, based on what you've been taught, do not exist. It's only a matter of perception and choice," explained Hhere.

Whew! I thought to myself. This was a lot of information, and I was getting tired. Concentrating within meditation is very draining. Hhere tells me to sleep and that our conversation will continue soon.

CHAPTER 11

HULLIGEN

May 6th, 2:11 a.m.

I returned to that white space again. The scene was so perfect that not even Hollywood, with all of its glamour, could duplicate such beauty. Again, I saw God poking holes into this huge black block that resembled a car engine, and wood was strewn all about. I wanted to ask what he was doing, but was too embarrassed. Seriously, why God would be working on a car engine was beyond me. I looked over to my left and saw nine white globes hovering in mid-air. The globes were more like planets, and I could sense that each of these globes had life within them. This was a spectacular site to see. While staring in amazement, I could feel Ccerdi standing behind me. She said in a motherly tone, "Look down." To my surprise, there was no floor, and it was like I was standing on top of the Milky Way. "Whoa!" I exclaimed like a little boy. Gazing down into bright stars and deep space, God showed me earth-like globes spiraling into infinity!

"We are constantly creating," said Ccerdi. Next, she moved from around back of me to the front and spoke sternly. "This brings us to another truth that has to be revealed. We have created a new and advanced Earth-like planet. This one will be called Hulligen."

After she said this, she flashed an image in my mind of Earth with the number 4.0 - meaning Hulligen would be highly advanced. "How will it be more advanced?" I asked.

"Hulligen will produce double the minerals and elements than your planet ever could. It's advanced because the life intelligence that will inhabit it will have a direct connection to God and not choose to be separated by inequities and concealment, like on your planet. In addition, all on Hulligen will live as one," Ccerdi said.

"Where is Hulligen located?"

Ccerdi replied, "Hulligen is in the constellation Cygnus, where its brightest star Deneb is located."

I don't know why, but I asked, "Can you give the coordinates of Hulligen in its star system?"

Note: Over a period of 10 minutes, I received some numbers. Admittedly, I don't know what they meant or if there was any accuracy to them. I'm not making any claim regarding whether these are coordinates; however, the following are the numbers that stood out: 73, 49, 80, 6, 704.

"Hmm, interesting… do our scientists know about this planet?" I asked.

God answered, "No, and they will not have access to it. You are the only and last man to have laid eyes on Hulligen."

Hhere/Ccerdi allowed me to view this new planet, yet only gave me 20 seconds to do so. The reason I was given only 20 seconds to view Hulligen was not to allow my external vibration as a human to corrupt the purity of Hulligen's virgin outer and inner atmosphere.

In the following vision, Hhere showed me an image of a lab within the dimension on earth where the Layonians live and work within this hybrid project. I saw a large hulk-like body in a liquid chamber.

Hhere pointed to the body in that chamber and continued to speak. "This body will be stronger and bigger and more advanced than what any man possesses on your world."

Confused as to what I was looking at, I didn't think to inquire as to what or whose body was suspended in that liquid chamber. "Hhere/Ccerdi?"

"Yes?" said God.

"What life intelligence will inherit Hulligen, and where will they come from? Will anyone from Earth get to go there?" I asked.

"This is a very important question, and we know the answer will not be an easy one to accept. The new life chosen will come from your planet and no other place; however, there will only be two species evolving from Earth to inherit Hulligen," Ccerdi said.

Challenging her, I said, "What do you mean, only two species?"

"I mean exactly that! The hybrid project on Earth, for reasons stated earlier, emerged as Homo sapiens. Earth's position is affected by the gravitational pull of its planetary family. This pulling effect slows down the physical vibration of the Homo sapiens, and all information contained within the identity of this species (e.g., ideas, emotions, physical movement, and choices) is expressed in even lower degrees to the point that these levels are almost unintelligible and crude. Now, the ascension begins. The intelligence within the body begins to wake up and remember who it really is, and it begins to choose how to express its truth in relationship to the other lower or higher experience that surrounds it (e.g., family relationships, politics). Ultimately, what will emerge from this highly complex soup of intelligence built within your species will give rise to another species that's better evolved socially and emotionally with each other. They will be more technologically advanced and perfectly balanced with Nature. Also, they will be respectful of their bodies and be directly connected with God," said Ccerdi.

"I'm not following you. What species is rising?" I was afraid to ask, "And you said it's only two?"

"There are two classifications: the Drixlb species and your plant species. The entire plant species from Earth is vital to the development and growth of Hulligen. The plant species and its new host will be interdependent on each other, thus creating ideal ecological environments. The Drixlb species is the evolved form of the Homo sapiens. Standing at about 7' to 8' tall, their dark-brown bodies are hairless, massive, and muscular and are enormously strong. However intimidating, their faces are soft and extremely charismatic. The prominent facial features are their dimples and beautiful smiles that are highlighted with comedic ears. The anatomy of their skin is highly durable to withstand the higher temperatures emitted from their star – Deneb. Also, their skin is porous and, when desired, can draw in large amounts of moisture. Socially, this species will love and accept all things as their level of enlightenment is six degrees higher than your Dalai Lama. The sexuality of a Drixlb is a full expression of love and compassion, yet without lasciviousness. Also, what you'll find interesting is that, physiologically, every Drixlb is born with both male and female reproductive systems. So, within a relationship, they simply choose what sexual role they want to experience and suffer neither shame nor prejudice. These are the only two species evolving from Earth," Ccerdi explained.

I'm overwhelmed with this information and don't know what to ask first. "I'm curious; will you explain further about the dual reproductive systems?" I asked.

"The physical design is quite remarkable and complex from a medical and scientific point of view. Happily and freely, a Drixlb simply chooses whatever sexual experience it wants to have and will receive no negative feedback from the immediate community. If a Drixlb wants to have a female experience, then it happily chooses that female reproductive function and birthing experience. Likewise, if a Drixlb wants to experience masculinity in reproduction, then it chooses that. This species is extremely advanced emotionally; therefore, by going through whatever sexuality it chooses, they also have a depth of understanding and compassion for their partners. Ultimately, true understanding of a partner creates an unbreakable bond, and communication between the two leaves no room for misunderstanding. Their love for each other is perfect," God said. "Also, I would like to point out that the complex and harmonious reproductive design of the Drixlb species was derived from the homosexual behaviors on your planet. Contrary to your fears and distortion, homosexuality is a designed action. One of the objectives of the alien project is to have humans engage in same-sex relationships. In addition, within the bounds of the project, aliens mesh themselves to your conscious space and experience these sexual acts with you. This conscious meshing is only achieved when the host, or human male or female, unknowingly chooses and allows a specific alien to mesh with them. This is a completely amicable relationship between the human host and alien. Besides, each person's existence on Earth is cemented in an agreement that life be expressed to its fullest. I will explain this agreement in detail shortly. Continuing, when a human of a particular sex feels the need to be involved with another of the same sex, they are not alone in such a decision. The sexual urges of a human host are empowered and intensified by the alien who is both meshed and desiring to have that sexual experience. Remember, as explained earlier, one of the objectives of the hybrid project was to allow the alien engineers to be able to experience, through mankind, the opposite of something they are not. There are distinct differences of a human host's desires within same-sex relationships versus what the aliens want. In a man/man or woman/woman relationship, there can be multiple reasons as to why someone chooses the have some type of sexual relationship with the same sex, ranging from psychological imbalance, childhood sexual abuse, or trauma, to a simple desire to indulge. Homosexuality is a lightning rod for heated arguments and dejection on your planet. As I said before, it is a misunderstood behavior. Next, the alien who wants to know what sex feels like through both heterosexual and/or homosexual relationships on Earth has an entirely different initiative. The alien's goal and loyalty is to the completion and perfection of the Hybrid project. For example, let me explain the sexual experience agreement between a human host and an alien. Currently, there's an alien group that is involved in the project whose males don't have genitalia, yet they're still involved in procreation on their planet in a way that you cannot comprehend. However, most of these alien males have a life question that burns in their souls, which is, *How do I know my masculine self, physically?* Next, you have a young human male, who is emotionally torn with the desire to be with another of the same sex. Yet he will undergo great stress and dejection from his parents, peers, religious leaders, or lawmakers who judge him as an outcast. Consequently, the troubled man's emotions begin to peak, and if not balanced, this stress could lead to greater illness in his life. However, the alien male monitors the situation and approaches the young man. A conversation ensues, and in short, the alien offers to help him. Once an agreement is made, the alien literally meshes his conscious energy with the consciousness of the man and begins to empower him with ideas and/or instills the courage to break away from opposing forces that seek to control him. Then, one day, the young man decides not to be afraid anymore and seeks to liberate himself, while at the same time allowing the alien male to know and feel his masculine self sexually. Ultimately, when the young man has expressed and is fulfilling his sexual truth, the alien also has expressed itself and then disconnects from the young man to his own cognizance. Finally, in the sexual triangle relationships of male/male/alien, male/female/alien, and female/female/alien, it doesn't matter for the alien within the project; it's simply a matter of experiencing, liberating, and evolving themselves and at the same time helping humans emotionally, psychically, and physically liberate themselves," God said.

I stared at God in disbelief, but at this point I totally believed and trusted what God was telling me. They could tell that my concentration was beginning to wane within my meditative state, so they told me to sleep, that there'd be more to the dialog on homosexuality, and that they would return the next evening to continue.

CHAPTER 12

DEEP GOD TALK

May 7, 2:15 a.m.

LYING in my sleeping bag on the living room floor, I rolled over onto my back and realized that my arms and ankles were unfolded. There are physical points within your chest area and at your joints of your ankles that are spiritual ports of entry. While sleeping, I knew that my spiritual ports were exposed and could feel the presence of God arriving. Lying on the floor awake, I heard God pick up where they left off the previous night.

"Chris, let us continue our dialog. Unfortunately, your societies frown upon homosexuality; however, none of them can explain what it is they're opposing. Those who point their finger in judgment are simply repeating what they heard from someone else. They can't think for themselves. In addition, those who preach in my name claim that I (God) abhor such an act, but I tell you this; I don't care, and I am not going to punish anyone who simply chooses to explore and love their bodies as they wish. This is why I allowed the aliens to create this hybrid project, so that they and the life created out of it can fully express every facet of their physical being. It is not in my interest to punish, condemn, or interfere with any of you exercising free will to love your bodies. All of you can do what you wish; it's your body!" exclaimed God "Next, there's a noticeable rise in the awareness and choosing of same-sex relationships. You're seeing it more and more throughout your private lives, in mass media, and in public places. This momentum is no coincidence, and it is the result of the expansion of the sexual triangle relationship involving humans and aliens. This sex relationship, and more specifically, homosexuality at its core, starts a process of negation. When a same-sex experience happens, it actually puts in motion a positive energy that begins to unravel or negate the person's life negative. I mention positive, because anyone who chooses their truth of how to express themselves is being positive, and the negatives are the buildup of lies, prejudices, shame, and pain gathered over time. These dramas [or globs of energy!] are often passed through from generation to generation, until one person decides to face his or her truth and acknowledge it. Aside from the lewd displays that are associated with some homosexual experiences, these nuances do not interfere with the real work that is being done at the crucial level of where consciousness meets the subconscious. Therefore, when a same-sex relationship begins, and because of the truth expressed and exposed, it puts in motion an energy that starts to reverse all the negatives that have been subjugated within them. Once again, all the negatives that are within a person are often life's negatives passed down from their ancestors, etc. Ultimately, as each generation becomes balanced with their sexuality, whether heterosexual or homosexual, each person will become more evolved. You must not forget that sex in fallacy is an axle that allows one to see into their future that will continually be webbed in hate and separation. However, sex in truth is the axle to where life is expanded in a future of love and compassion. This form of enlightenment leads people to want to fix the inequities among humanity and to correct the imbalance with nature. Ergo, this is how the dual sexuality of the Drixlb was perfected, through the great strides all of you are taking within embracing your sexuality and growing from that experience." God explained.

"Thank you for that explanation. I'm curious – will Earth be used to populate any other planets, in or around our Solar System?" I asked.

From inside the Holy synergy, Hhere speaks. "No, the Earth project was for the creation and development of species that'll inherit Hulligen. Your race will not be used for any other colonization."

"When will Hulligen host its new guest?"

"The Drixlb species will inhabit Hulligen in 2014. It's imperative to note as to what will bring the Drixlb body to life, since our conversation mentioned only the physical aspects of this new species. Shortly before the year 2014, your nation will suffer an unbearable catastrophe, and because of this, in 2014 there'll be a first mass movement of souls that will migrate from your planet to Hulligen. These souls will then take possession of the Drixlb bodies, spark them to life, and begin life as Drixlbs. This first migration will mark the first step toward the totality of mankind's complete transformation to becoming a Drixlb," replied God. Ccerdi moved out of their synergy. "Now, there's a difficult cross-road that your race faces, and this is the challenge to evolve higher from your current position in life. Though you have been engineered with alien/primate DNA- at some level this would suggest that you don't have control over whom and what you become. However, this is furthest from the truth. The fact is that your consciousness powers each of you to be involved; furthermore, at another level, all of you completely understand who you are and what has been going on, yet, you've chosen not to remember. The tedious engineering of the Drixlb body was a collaboration between me (my will), alien intelligence, and to a degree the intuitive force that vibrates within the primates and you. Therefore, there were four players involved in the highly complex project on your planet. This project has multiple objectives to it. One goal was to ensure that every man and woman has the wherewithal and power of freewill. While based on a person's choice and movement, the aliens were allowed to begin engineering the body of the Drixlb species. When people came together and started to have inter-racial relations and intermarried with one another, your exploration of cultures and exchanging of ideas were vital for the successful physical design. Then there was a turning point for your entire race. Man decided to charter his own path and moved away from the agreement with his other co-creators of the project. By moving away from this core group, he jeopardized his assured divine protection. It is obvious that humanity has done well with the building of great societies, but without this divine protection, his spiritual nature has been exposed to something highly dangerous – Satan – contrary to status, technology, power, and intelligence. Moving away from divine protection not only put humanity under the control of Satan, but his perversions upon your race have deduced all of you to become something unintelligible. Future generations will become so un-evolved that society will undermine everything I have created for Earth and Hulligen. "

Listening intently, I asked, "Then how is this problem to be corrected?"

"Xzabea explained to you earlier that her race engineered the brown-skinned people within certain regions of your world. Rising from the southern regions that are now identified as the Central Americas was an intelligent culture that had a specific class of people who were aware and privy to information about the Layonians and the hybrid project on your planet. This early class was made up of religious, royal, and tribal leaders; they were taught about the development of the future man. In addition, while the Layonians educated this group about their true origins and gave them technology and science, they also taught them how to mark the time of the future man. Ironically, they were also given an end date for his world. During the transmission of information, there was much confusion as to why I would mark an end date for mankind, before he fully arose, the reason was simple; I saw how quickly man's consciousness became autonomous and knew that at some point I would have to thwart his will power. Then a dichotomy arose: how to allow the project to naturally progress, which the soul of Man was still very much a part of, and when and how to intervene in the self-destructive course that was foreseen? With much calculation, I picked a moment in time, (2012), that would mark the divine interference of man's growth and an introduction of a new life union on Earth. The union between man and alien will allow the hybrid project to progress naturally and also serve to protect the future man from being completely destroyed by Satan. Starting in 2013, this human/ alien relationship will last one-thousand-years and huge a conscientious move on man's part to forever separate from dark tethers that bounded him. However, any real change to evolve must have the assistance of alien intelligence who understands the path away from Satan. This transformative period is not only for modern man, but for the aliens as well. Yours is not the only reality that suffers inequities and troubles; the alien level also has its share of chaos." Ccerdi fluctuates in and out of the physical. "I just mentioned that your world will be undergoing a massive transformation of the mind and soul. This divine lift will awaken the rulers of people and a collective effort will be in order to bring up those less fortunate than they. Worldwide hatred and prejudice will become an embarrassing black eye of your past. Your world will be evolved! Ccerdi says, while appearing to look right through me. "At the height of world harmony, a second and final catastrophic blow will befall your planet and this will create a second mass movement of souls. Hundreds of millions of human souls will leave Earth and travel along a protected path to Hulligen. Each will take possession a Drixlb body, further propagating that species to greater futures. When this spiritual migration is completed - this period will mark the finality for all mankind and his Earth." I struggle to see Ccerdi, as she is fading like mist. Her voice seems more distant. "There will be a great question in future history books: What happened to modern man? The answer will be, "Modern man has made the difficult metamorphosis and great transformation from Homo sapiens to a highly evolved species called-Drixlb, and Earth is no more." Ccerdi stepped back into the synergy.

While I sat listening to God speak, a cloud of disbelief and cynicism came over me. I stood up and said, "How do I know if you're really God or if this is some trick of the devil?" All of a sudden, they got quiet, and like someone shutting off the lights, the entire scene around me went dark. It was eerie! Two images appeared before me, one to the right and the other to the left. Then I heard God say, "You can continue down the path of desolation, pain, and loss, or you can take the path of higher knowledge – choose one!" they said. One image projected a landscape of misery and pain. The other image was of a white path with beautiful trees that radiated protection. Feeling truth, I chose the latter and held my head down. I felt strongly that I had been about to make a grave mistake if I had not chosen the path of higher knowledge.

At some point I started crying, because I realized that I was about to mess up the opportunity of a lifetime of having a face-to-face dialog with God. To further console me, Ccerdi took a droplet of water and placed it on one of the wooden boards that were lying near the engine Hhere was working on. I walked over to see what she was doing and it read, "I love you, Son!" Realizing that I was back in the white space with God, I asked where I was. God made an odd noise that didn't even qualify as a sound. I struggled to listen and noticed that the sound was fine tuning itself into a frequency or words that I could understand. Then I heard this, "You are standing in the realm of the Immaculate Absolute." I listened in amazement and then noticed that God had formed into a massive sphere of energy that whisked high in the universe. They were illustrating that they sit far beyond any dust particle, cloud, star, planet, or other matter in space. At the lower left-hand corner of this illustration, there was dark blue gas that dissipated as it spread up toward God's realm. In addition, within the same demonstration, God was also saying that they sit well beyond any thought of mankind. This was illustrated at the lower right-hand side of this picture, with a tree with sprawling branches that failed to reach God. Then they re-appeared with me standing in their realm of the Immaculate Absolute. Hhere approached me with two God symbols: one was a medallion with a live black hole, and around the circumference it had three gold clovers fanning out from the dark hole. This meant that life comes from the void. The second God mark was a circle with strange lines around it, yet in the middle of this mark was the number 6 facing another number 6 facing backwards. It was like the 6 was facing itself in a mirror. This represented both Hhere and Ccerdi and their respective male/female aspects. The message from this mark was that they are inseparable and create as one. They are the Creators of all life.

My conversation this night with God was exhausting, and I had a difficult time maintaining my concentration during meditation. Seeing that I was losing focus, Ccerdi ended our meeting and stated that there was another truth that had to be revealed; they'd return tomorrow night to continue their conversation. Then I fell into a heavy slumber.

CHAPTER 13

HUETPHER

WOW, I thought to myself. *I must have been really exhausted, because I slept through all of Friday and that evening.* I could have slept longer, but I was awakened by the neighbor bumping his car speakers loudly. I felt agitated, because it was Friday night and it was time for partying, and I too wanted to go out and have some fun. But I was broke. Ain't got no money and no car! I once heard this line from a girl: No money, no honey! However, I kept my emotions in check and prevented myself from getting depressed. At this point in my life, I accepted what came my way.

In an effort at least to get out of the house, I walked up to my local Chinese restaurant and stuffed my face with Singapore noodles.

The evening wore on, and I sat on the living room floor with my back against the wall. I didn't think about anything, I just wanted to relax. Letting my mind drift, that evening's dinner was my only thought. I could still smell remnants of curry around my mouth. With a full stomach, I got what we called in the black community- the Itis. Luckily, my sleeping bag was just an arm's length away. Just a few moves to the right and I was tucked in nicely and fell asleep. Feeling a soft hand on my chest, I awakened to find myself sitting in the Realm of the Absolute with God standing off to my right.

"Hello Chris," God said.

Physically I felt groggy from my previous night's dinner and my heavy sleep. Still clearing my eyes and not wanting to be rude, I managed to speak. "Umph, morning," I said.

Without wasting time, Ccerdi walked over to me. "Remember earlier when you saw Hhere look into that vertical band of energy, and you asked what it was?"

"Yes, he said that he was monitoring man," I responded

Ccerdi stared at me intensely. "Let me cover another aspect of that energy strand and reveal another truth to be told. Completely surrounding your planet and permeating all life, there's a single living intelligence. This intelligence contains 12 dimensions within it. The physical structure that holds this intelligence and dimensions in place are your trees. The tree in your backyard is part of something quite extraordinary."

I wiped my eyes to wake up. "Will you explain further?"

"What I'm about to explain to you will be given in two part. This first part will give a general overview of the information I'm to share with you, and the second dialog will be extensive information for your second book." Ccerdi told me. "The living intelligence surrounding and permeating every life form on your planet is called a Huetpher. The best way to describe a Huetpher is that it's like a single thought or idea of God. Similar to each of you that has an idea about your family or work, etc., within your single thought there is great information and multiple dimensions and possibilities. This is the same for us; the Huetpher is a single idea of God, and within it are twelve dimensions. These dimensions are live and functioning, yet they do not mix. They range in a descending order, with the twelfth as the highest and one as the lowest. Ten of the twelve levels are soul dimensions. If you ever wanted to know where your soul goes when you die and where it currently vibrates while in the living, it's in one of these levels. Two of the twelve dimensions are actually physical realities. The physical reality of mankind and the other physical reality that parallels your world are where the aliens are currently located. Now, let me give brief description of each level: The dimensions range from high to low. The twelfth level is the soul and conscious vibration of Christ. It is the most pure and is heavily protected, as nothing and no one can enter it. Each dimension less the twelfth begins to slow in vibration and begins to coagulate with dark matter. Subsequently, the lower 3 dimensions are so dark; their vibration is considered the conscious vibration of the anti- Christ. Now, Chris, to demonstrate what each of these dimensions looks like, I want you to use your gift to see what I'm saying," Ccerdi said.

While Ccerdi spoke, I focused on her words and followed its frequency to see the actual Huetpher and its twelve dimensions. The Huetpher has a light tan coloration and a thick density. It wraps itself around our world, and I could feel that it moved through any and all living specimen in our soil. Next, I saw the twelve dimensions in a position like a flat pancake. In this flat position, all of the dimensions looked like the rings on a tree stump. Then, like a slinky being pulled up, all of the twelve dimensions stretched up so that I could see the whole clearly. Interestingly, Ccerdi said: the higher the level, the more it vibrates in the Christ Consciousness and lower levels become dense in a Satan vibration. Even in coloration, the extremes can be seen, the highest soul dimension was white and pure, and each level below it darkened to various shades of grey to pure black. When I focused on the twelfth, there was a massive gold angel guarding the entrance. It is there to protect the soul/ conscious vibration of Christ from all lesser and foreign spiritual frequency that seeks to corrupt and imbalance it. There are serious consequences if any breach of the Christ dimension is attempted- not even Satan himself tampers with it. Interestingly, while I continued to view the twelfth, I noticed on its floor hundreds of fat and happy babies from all races. While amused at this scene, Ccerdi explained that the twelfth dimension is where all of our souls initially came from. However, she also told me that none of us can ever re-enter it and that we only come from it once. But, there's a single caveat for a human soul to re-enter the twelfth dimension: Any soul incarnation during early infancy that loses its life is instantly whisked to this divine safe haven. However, Ccerdi stressed the point that the physical age determination for an infant's soul to re-enter the twelfth dimension is at twelve months or less. Beyond the twelve month, if that soul loses its physicality, then the current vibration (continuation from prior experiences) or level is where its stays until it chooses to re-incarnate in its future. Next, I looked down to the eleventh dimension. This realm we can also not enter, as it is reserved for the souls of animals. How fascinating that the next and highest soul vibration and closest to Christ vibration are animals! *Hmm*, I murmured, *I think Man has things backwards to who's really dominant.* Ccerdi stopped me here and told me that, of all souls at this level, the soul of a dog is their most favorite! This was illustrated by a gorgeous golden retriever standing next to a bunch of vibrant green trees and the branches of the trees with happily shaking leaves reaching down and petting the dog's neck and fur! Ccerdi went on to tell me that a dog's soul possesses the highest vibration of all animals on our world; its vibration is closest to the purity of Christ. I understood Ccerdi in saying that dogs exemplify the greatest act of loyalty and love toward its owner, regardless of how bad a life it has been given.

Curious, I skipped the tenth dimension and sought to see the physical reality that parallels ours. Our dimension within the Huetpher sits at the sixth position, and the other reality is the ninth. This one sits directly above ours and is occupied by the Layonians and other alien life forms that monitor their project. Ccerdi explained that this is how they can move in and out of our realm, because they sit above us. The ninth dimension was fascinating and, while this may be hard to believe, from what I could tell, there are 3 or 4 super-science complexes. A single complex covers North American and South American continents, and others span the entire continents of Europe, and Africa. I couldn't see clearly how the other continents were connected, but they were. It was like some auxiliary or smaller-scaled facilities. It was shown to me that these mega-complexes could comfortably house a few billion human beings. The design of these super structures is intricately meshed and connected with the trees on our physical level. This design allows the aliens to move easily in and out of our space. The complexity of this design is so clever that, other than traveling through our trees, aliens can move about through any type of vegetation, brush, or bush. At first as I listened and saw the explanation of how they move in and out of our reality, I couldn't truly register how they physically transport through an actual tree and brush. At some level, I concluded that it was an unseen dimensional aspect, yet I still wanted more information on this issue. To satisfy my inquiry, God showed me that, within the tree and its space, there are flexible metal tunnels that can bend to the sways of the tree itself. These tunnels serve as the connection and throughway between the sixth and ninth dimensions. Also, these mega structures are connected by enormous waterways that link from one structure to another and also link down into our oceans and seas.

However, the aliens prefer flight from one structure to another.

These unique complexes were purposely built to serve the alien intelligences that specialize in areas of science and technology. As I had mentioned before, Xzabea told me that it was aliens that helped our civilized societies emerge into super power by empowering them with great technology. Ccerdi explained this in detail. She said that one of several alien projects that operate out of this super science structure is identified as L.A.R. This acronym stands for Layonian, American, and Russian. This is a joint force that involves both human and alien cooperation. In brief, this coalition serves two primary objectives: Advanced Species engineering and Human Technology Assistance.

The two primary recipients of great technology were America and Russia; ultimately, this agreement was solidified to what is known as L.A.R. The L.A.R. coalition is still intact, however, not as strong. New coalitions are now beginning to be formed with other nations on our planet and the rising projects are Science and Ecology.

For example, Ccerdi showed me one of the current objectives of L.A.R.: A new jet technology has been given that will allow man to fly in and out of space into Earth's atmosphere with great ease and no heat or structural damage to the craft. In addition, the technology will basically allow our fighter jets to fly from ground to space without complex and bulky launch pads. Ccerdi showed me that this L.A.R. flight technology is operating under a one-person test project here in North America. The tests are conducted in the dark of night, taking place near the

Washington Cascade range. Ccerdi mentioned that it was close to Mt. Rainer. I focused closely and could see a small and abandoned-looking Quonset hut attached with a tattered-looking carport, all covered in ice. But this was a decoy. That hut houses one of the most advanced aircraft ever conceptualized. It was explained that its technology is 150 years advanced over any aircraft on the planet.

My mind and heart were racing with excitement to witness this phenomenon. Curious about something she had said earlier, I asked why the aliens needed permission and cooperation from man to execute their project, especially if it was purported that they engineered us. Why did they need our approval?

Ccerdi moved back into the divine synergy with Hhere. "When humans became aware of themselves, the Layonians needed permission and cooperation from the awakened to continue developing their alien/primate hybrid project. It was important to seek permission, as not to impose upon the self-awakening of man. The engineering project had to continue without disruption; therefore, it adapted to this new course of action. Because the Layonians and their other intelligent cohorts needed their hybrid plan to develop slowly, they were highly selective among man, with whom they sought cooperation. The principles of the alien project involved the selection of people who displayed greater levels of comprehension and influence over others. Therefore, cooperation was sought with intellectuals and elitists who had control and influence over the masses and powerful establishments, and alien technology was given to them. Even to this day, the aliens still seek cooperation with those on your planet who display greater comprehension and influence. Free will is never disrupted."

Further exploring these super-science complexes on the ninth dimension, I learned that each has a large landing area for large space crafts to stage on. In addition, these white and vast structures contain large operation centers that are used for observing the day-to-day operations of the complex; in addition, each has an operations division whose the sole goal is to monitor life on our sixth dimension. Each alien monitor is tasked to a specific agenda that ranges from identifying individual behavioral pattern to observing a specific race and how they are communicating and responding with other people. Some are tasked to connect with humans and assist in their growth. Outside these massive alien complexes, the landscape looked like the beautiful country of the Dominican Republic. Amazingly, there were crystal clear, turquoise-colored lakes and healthy palm trees that stretched for miles and miles. I don't know how far this gorgeous landscape reached, but with each viewing, I kept seeing the same tranquil setting.

I'd explored dimensions twelve, eleven, and nine. These are the levels that none of us can occupy, and the sixth level is where we live. Now, this leaves dimensions; ten, eight, seven, five, four, three, two, and one. Remember that these are the only dimensions that we can vibrate within. Also, as a reminder, that the higher the level, the closer that soul vibrates in Christ Consciousness. The tenth and eighth dimensions are in rare company. The souls that vibrate in that space are unique; they represent a group that focuses entirely on uplifting others. These souls live a life that is total sacrifice for the whole. They are comprised of both public, famous, and private people. Interestingly, the soul vibration of private men and women are the majority within one of these high dimensions. Their career fields range from religion to business. These people have divine like qualities, and this shows through their work and commitment to uplift all of mankind. Most work in ignored sections; a city's communities and others are pioneers of industry. It doesn't matter the size of their contribution, just that there is great movement of advancement of a people. For example, I saw the soul vibration of Mother Theresa in the tenth dimension. Factually, the tenth level is the highest that any human being can occupy. The difference between the tenth and eighth levels are minor degrees of vibration; whereas, the tenth dimension directive is responsible for a large number of souls to be uplifted, while the eighth level requires progression on a smaller scale.

In the follow up book to this subject of the Huetpher, more detail will be covered about the uniqueness of the tenth and eighth dimensions, because at these realms souls can choose to stay where they are at or to come back into the physical. Whatever way it chooses - the dimension main directive has to be executed. Those who come back to the earthly experience chooses their specific physical experience along with other souls who agree to come with and live out their agreed upon scenario- while the souls who chose to stay in spiritual dimension provide assistance or guidance when called upon. When a soul chooses the physical realm, each can choose what race, gender, motive, place, parents, etc., it will get. Souls choose what is needed to raise their vibrations. Some souls eventually vibrate higher, but some souls actually fail and vibrate at a lower level. *Note: Actually, it isn't the soul who failed, it's the conscious person who chose not to listen to their soul and chose wrongly or poorly. In addition, whatever negative thoughts, acts, deeds, or perversions are committed by the person in the physical, these energies attach itself to the good vibration of the soul. Thus, the soul's pure and white vibration becomes weighted down with black spots of negativity.*

The next dimension explored is the seventh; this level is the most difficult for souls to get beyond. At some earlier point in time, all souls vibrated below the seventh realm, and had to begin their ascent. Unlike the other dimensions to where souls can stay or come back to physical, the seventh realm requires all souls that vibrate at this l degree to be in the flesh. It is here that the seventh directive commands a soul to present to its physical host the opportunity to sacrifice something of great importance to them – even their life if required – for the betterment and rise of another. It doesn't matter what path a soul takes at the physical realm, as long at this challenge is met. The seventh dimension presents a single and difficult question to answer: What can you sacrifice of yourself for the uplift of someone else? Unfortunately, many souls cannot get beyond this point, due to their pathological thoughts and shallow heart. Sadly, a soul can experience many lifetimes and opportunities to ascend their position within the Huetpher, and when they reach the seventh dimension, it's easy to assume they will continue their spiritual rise. However, at this level, if a soul's life question isn't answered correctly, then its vibratory state becomes dense and begins a rapid descent to lower dimensions.

The next levels are the fifth and fourth- both are a low vibration.

However, these two levels are in a unique position, because both dimensions sit at a pivot within the Huetpher. At a certain point within the Huetpher there's a natural movement that spirals upward or center, not downward or away, ultimately providing for these souls an extra lift toward their ascension. This energetic and upward momentum of the Huetpher translates into *spiritual assistance*. Generally, people whose souls vibrate at fifth or fourth dimensions have a laboring life; laboring due to self-sabotage of happiness. Each is susceptible to doing wrong when they know to do right. Yet to these souls credit they put forth good effort to be a better person overall. The quiet trait each person has – whose souls vibrate in five or four dimensions - is the act of being conscientious. Even more, the ability to take in humility, allows that person to receive spiritual assistance from the Huetpher. Like a surfer catching a great wave, when a person becomes aware of a good or truth about a situation, becoming conscientious about it – that mental vibration wave attaches itself to the natural upswing of the Huetpher and begins a slow rise. At this level and more than others, paying close attention to one's conscious is vital, because trying to do the right things in life for themselves means also trying to do right for something larger than itself.

Ccerdi explained the business of souls in this way. In general, what must be understood is that your soul isn't yours per se. It's a continuation of others' lives within your family lineage. The soul arrives as pure, balanced, and intelligent, but as it experiences life on earth it becomes tainted with negative matter. The acts and words and deeds of its host (human) are converted into low vibratory energy. This foreign energy is not welcomed, so the soul begins to formulate a question: How do I correct this situation? It wants to get back to its original and pure self. This soul chooses its physical experiences or path in an attempt to resolve its life question. Every person walking on this planet has life questions, such as Who am I? What is my expression in the world? What is my relationship to my parents? There are many life questions that souls set out to answer. Unfortunately, the poor soul has to rely on the fickle person whose mind is usually preoccupied with self-centeredness and prejudice. Thus, the opportunity to have its life question resolved is unfruitful. The soul will travel the physical many times until it finds the right person, one who has the patience to listen and the courage to answer its life question. In the majority of cases, a soul picks up multiple life questions, due to a reckless person who abused their life. What's even more horrible is that, as the soul comes into life over and over again, each human host will let him or her down, further injecting more negativity. Ultimately, and after a few dozen lifetimes, a soul has its life question(s) answered and begins its ascension to the higher dimensions. Therefore, the souls that are vibrating at levels five and four are in easier and greater positions to answer their life questions, thus saving time and pain for someone else in the future to have to carry that burden.

After Ccerdi spoke, Hhere interjected, saying they wanted me to pay close attention to the lower dimensions of three, two, and one. These three realms are the lowest and vibrate in the Satan consciousness. The coloration of these levels ranged from black to pitch black. Strangely, the first dimension was so dark that there was a thick, oily residue oozing from within the black matter. Admittedly, I became disturbed by what I saw and couldn't go into these dimensions. Fear swept through me when I saw people's souls sadistically intertwined with something that couldn't be described. In these black realms, many souls had (consciously) chosen to be there and were addicted to torment, sexual abuse, pain, and any drama grounded in fear. In addition, a large number of souls who vibrate in the first dimension have made blood pacts with Satan for power and fortune.

Hhere/ Ccerdi wanted me to see these lower dimensions from their perspective and flashed an image of Earth. At about 1,000 feet from our ground surface, there was a thick black veil that connected every nation together, and there was no light within it. This dark energy at the lowest dimensions represents the collective consciousness of every person on this planet, indicating that 80% of the lives on our planet are unaware that their souls are in a dangerous place. Despite a person's flowery attempt to be close to God in song, word, or prayer, at the end of the day, Satan corrupts, manipulates, perverts, and claims their souls. Satan wants 100% control of the planet, and his agenda is almost complete. Furthermore, he has such a stronghold on mankind that any effort to pull away from him is close to impossible.

Alarmed by what I had heard, I asked for further explanation. God re-explained something that was mentioned earlier. She told me that, at some point within the alien project and at an indiscernible level of consciousness, man became aware of his self and broke away from the agreement with his other co-creators within the project. This action jeopardized his assured divine protection, and he instantly became ignorant. First, there was a loss of understanding about the way of life. Respect for our planet's natural balance and order also meant understanding the spiritual flow that exists. Near the subtle conscious vibration, the co-partners of the project were a foreign element here on earth. However, these foreign elements were coded with an intelligent cell that allowed it to coexist with the physical and spiritual aspects of our planet. Part of this instinctive understanding was about the importance of being connected with the intuitive spirit that permeated all of life. In addition, this intricate relationship with this spirit meant total protection from external physical elements that were not harmonious and meant to remain dormant. Unfortunately, when man took charge of his life, two problems presented itself: First, when Man became aware of God and could not grasp the enormity of this omnipresence, he compounded his ineptness by further distancing himself and created great concealment to the truth about God's true aspect. Secondly, when the lie about God was committed, early man became seduced by the lusciousness of Earth's loam. Thus, materialism became his obsession.

While listening to Ccerdi speak, I realized that my dialog with Hhere/Ccerdi would soon end, and I made a personal decision to serve them in any way I could.

"Chris, we've given you much information and have revealed secrets to be told. Also, we are going to instruct you how to connect with the Huetpher. We are going to teach you how to identify the ninth dimension and make contact with the aliens who await all of mankind. Then, we are going to teach you how to identify your individual soul amongst the multiple dimensions and how to ascend to higher levels." She looked at me with intensity. "Understanding the Huetpher will not be easy, and often times it will be precarious; yet this path is vital toward correct evolution. Over the next three days, you'll receive instructions, and when completed and when you fully comprehend the Huetpher, our desire for you is to teach others about this wonderful phenomenon that all of you are very much part of. Will you deliver our message? Will you teach this?" Ccerdi asked.

I responded eagerly, "Yes, I would do anything you'd ask of me!"

"Good," Ccerdi said. "Before we go, there's one more truth to be revealed   his name is Touve" (Pronounced "T-ah-vay"). "You'll meet him soon."

Over the next few days, some Layonians came and gave instruction on how to connect and operate within the Huetpher. However fascinating it was to explore this intelligence with twelve dimensions, I had to admit that I was afraid to explore it because of the many unknowns it presented.

The following week was uneventful regarding communication with aliens and God, but I did receive some great news. A few months earlier, I had submitted an application to a trucking company to become a driver, and they called me and offered me a job. I was elated, and I felt that maybe my life was finally turning in my favor. Then it hit me – this job opportunity is more than some random, coincidental opportunity. I thought back to an earlier scenario with Hhere working on that large engine block, and upon contemplation, I realized that it was symbolic and God's way of saying, "I've heard your prayers and understand what you need; therefore, I'm sending you the right job for your highest needs." So, I analyzed how this job was the best for me in the moment. Obviously, it was an opportunity to start earning money again; yet, it was also way for me to heal. I didn't realize that a young female Layonian was sitting quietly next to me, and she helped me understand Hhere's engine symbolism. "God wants to re-acclimate you back into life. You didn't realize, but you were deliberately stripped of anything that preoccupied your attention, and this included the people closest to you.

Your physical vibration had to be free from outside disturbances, which allowed you to concentrate on the multiple experiences that kept reoccurring. This particular job to drive trucks will put you back in the fray of your busy world. In addition, God is aware that your living arrangement is temporary, and soon you'll need somewhere to stay. Therefore, driving a large tractor with a full cab speaks for itself," this small alien said.

My new career as a trucker had begun. I changed from wearing fine suits and expensive Johnston and Murphy shoes to wearing khakis and steel-toed boots.

CHAPTER 14

TOUVE

THROUGHOUT the summer and fall months of 2010, I drove around 15,000 average miles per month. Though it was for small pay, I was appreciative to have something in hand. I was driving on I-40 E one night, traveling through New Mexico, when I had the sudden urge to sleep. I got to a rest area to take a nap. Most truckers can fight through the fatigue, but I couldn't and did not want to risk a wreck or harm to myself. I pulled over to sleep for 30 minutes. After five minutes into sleep, I awakened to see a palatial hall. The magnificent structure had an institutional feel and featured massive ceiling-to-floor windows that looked out into the universe. Completely enamored by this site, I looked down to the assembly floor and saw a large round table. There must have been a hundred or more alien dignitaries sitting about, and I even saw Xzabea sitting there too. I could hear their chatter, as this meeting was held to discuss some very important upcoming event on Earth. Also, the assembly was also waiting for the arrival of someone very important.

My focus shifted, and I found myself standing behind three male aliens. The three were standing side by side and standing on a conservative dark purple carpet, ready to walk down a long and dark corridor with light blue sconces that lit the walls. The three were important figures, yet the one in the middle was the most important entity, and it was he that the assembly was waiting for. Standing on the left and right sides of the tall alien, the smaller males had white skin, and their physiques were similar to that of Xzabea's. Their heads and limbs were in good proportion to their bodies, and their eyes were pitch black and large. All three males wore long, smart-looking black capes that draped to the floor. The royal, tall alien was striking. His skin color was also white, and his head was shaped like the E.T. character from the Steven Spielberg movie; yet his face wasn't flat, as it protruded forward aggressively. His eyes were massive and black. He had a small nose and a small mouth with piranha-like teeth. The tall one was being escorted down a dark and regal hallway. While watching them walk, I took a closer look at the tall alien; the back of his head has a membrane connected to the back of his skull. The membrane wasn't discolored or deformed, displaying the same coloration as his skin. Mesmerizingly, as the tall one walked, from the fissures of his external membrane a copper-colored vapor flowed from it and all around him. Next, I saw the important entity step out onto a loft and to address those who sat around the round table. When he stepped out and looked down, the entire assembly hall erupted in jubilee and praise. Every alien, including Xzabea, shouted his name with great exaltation: "Touve! Touve! Touve!" The atmosphere was collegiate and passionate. I have to admit, it was quite impressive.

Moments later, I found myself sitting before Touve in his private chamber. Sitting on a small wooden stool, Touve sat humbly in a dark grey robe with a large hood that draped around his face. All I could see was his mouth, yet I could tell that he could see me through the hood. We both sat and looked at each other without saying a word. Breaking the silence, I said, "I was told I would be meeting you. My name is Chris." However, Touve said nothing.

He sat quietly, and finally said, "I've walked all over your planet and even drove your highways throughout North America. I like New York City."

I said, "You do?"

"Yes. I like New York, because of the mix of people. This is good!" says Touve.

"I also like Druid Hill Park!" he said.

"Where's that?" I asked.

"It's in Baltimore, Maryland. It's one of several parks I frequent on your planet," explained Touve. "Also, I like pizza from Italy."

During several conversations with this reclusive alien entity, I would often notice that some of his subjects would serve him his meal, and it would be brought in on a platter that looked like a pizza pan. Amused, I thought to myself that it looked like pizza they'd bring in to him. *Aliens don't eat pizza... do they?*

"Also, I like fried chicken!" said Touve.

I laughed. "My man, I do too!"

"I also like big fat biscuits and popcorn," Touve exclaimed.

What Touve said next made me chuckle for a week. "I like your drink concoction, gin and juice!"

Apparently, I had been talking to a very important alien being with access to some of the finest liquors on this planet, but he liked a cheap drink such as this. I laughed out loud. "Well, I'm not much of a drinker, but I've heard that it can get your head right!"

Touve roared in laughter!

I sensed the right moment to ask again. "Who are you?"

This mysterious alien's demeanor changed from jovial to serious. "My race is called Etos, and I'm from the constellation Aquila," Touve explained. "The galaxy I'm from is what you call Iras, and you'll recognize this galaxy for its yellow nebulae that is spatial within that part of the universe. The name of my planet is Chagon" (pronounced SHAH-gon).

Touve then told me to use my gift to view his planet. When I saw it, perhaps because of where his planets sit in close proximity to the yellow nebulae, the sky as well as the mountain terrain had a yellow hue. The green and yellow brush and rusty-colored soil reminded me of the landscape of Tucumcari, New Mexico. Then Touve showed me his planet from a distance, with a few hundred brilliant stars as a backdrop. Characteristically, his planet has no clouds around it, and the skies are always clear.

While I was looking at it, Touve spoke. "That's my planet, and it's as lonely as Druid Hill Park; just like my planet, no one visits it anymore."

I took a moment to contemplate the magnitude of this statement and the behavioral similarities between what he suggests between aliens and humans. The rich vegetation and perfumes from exotic flowers and beautiful old trees of that once-frequented park probably reminded him of his plant and the herbal characteristics of his world. Ergo, both alien and human had grown away from their nature and beauty and quietude in exchange for external ventures and other preoccupying vices.

There were many questions that raced through my mind. "Who are you specifically?" I asked.

"I'm ancient royalty; as a matter of fact, I'm very rare and ancient royalty. You've seen my royal signature, the copper-colored vapor permeating from the back of my skull. This is called an Etav; it is the mark of universal royalty of the most rare," Touve explained. "I sit directly under God." He paused to let me catch up.

When I heard him say he sits under God, I became confused. But before I could ask for clarification, Touve said, "I sit directly under God. I'm lateral to God's highest angels, yet not higher than Jesus Christ. I only report to God. From my domain, I control and rule over every constellation within the Milky Way. All of life – including all of you on your planet – has a part of me in you. Life springs from me! Spirit sparks from me! My mark has been stamped upon many, many worlds. This ancient royal mark, the Etav, you simply know as melanin!"

My mind was still processing this information, yet I had to remain focused. "What is your specific role in the significant event that is to take place on our planet soon?"

"I'm here to prepare you," Touve said.

"Prepare me for what?" I asked.

"I'm here to prepare you for the second coming of Christ!"

CHAPTER 15

SAINT MARY

DECEMBER 19, 2010, 3:23 p.m. The drive through part of northern California's landscape that shares the Sierra Nevada, along with Lake Tahoe, has become one of my favorite routes among all of my travels. I'm not partial to any cold climate, but there's something special about this area, with its snowcapped mountains and dark green massive pines powdered with light snow. Stressed from wrestling with 74,000 pounds of truck and loaded trailer, I pulled over to a rest area to stretch my legs and take in some fresh air. After strolling for 30 minutes, I decided to go back in the sleeper and take a nap. Within an hour, I awoke to see something strange near the foot of my bunk. There were some bundle of clothing near my feet, and after yawning and rubbing my eyes, I saw something penetrating through and sitting atop that mound of clothes. The image looked like the image of St. Mary, yet, I didn't think much of it. Staring at this peculiar image, it was becoming more apparent that my eyes were not deceiving me! The image of Virgin Mary was positioned near my feet. Clearly, I was looking at her black over garment and inner white hood draping the sides of her delicate ivory face and praying hands. I moved slowly so that I would not disturb this image, and when I got closer, it was still there. Sitting up slowly and planting my feet on the floor, I said a prayer to St. Mary and asked her to what I owed her visit? But there was no response of any kind. I asked the same question again, and still received no response from St. Mary. When I finished praying, I opened my eyes only to find that she had disappeared. I stared at the bundle of clothing to see if she would return, but nothing else happened. My thoughts of that strange occurrence left me with no words, and all I could do was contemplate that seemingly bizarre yet divine moment.

CHAPTER 16

WINTER SOLSTICE

WHILE traveling throughout the state of Washington, I heard on AM radio that there was an upcoming lunar eclipse on the December 21. There was much buzz about this celestial event on all the major online news media outlets, so my interest had been piqued, and I made it a point to mark this event on my phone calendar.

It was late in the evening as I drove on the icy highway of I-90 East traveling through Montana. My driver-side mirror displayed a temperature of 13 degrees Fahrenheit. Pushing 65mph, my drive foot was stuck to the gas pedal and numb due to the cold that was blowing through the bottom of my door. The evening became more laboring, as I was lulled by the quiet night freeze as I struggled against the fatigue brought on by the monotony of the road. I couldn't remember anything within 10 seconds of passing an object, and then, like the brassy bugle call of reveille, my Blackberry phone's calendar alert rang out! Jarring me out of hypnotism, I grabbed the phone, irritated, to see why I had an alert that early in the morning.

I forgot that I had set a reminder to see the lunar eclipse for December 21 at around 1:00 a.m. MDT, so I quickly began to look for a safe place to park. Finally, arriving at a safe spot to park, I jumped out of the truck and looked up to the night sky. My timing was perfect, because I caught the eclipse in its full totality! This was a spectacular event to witness. The moon had a gorgeous amber color as the Earth blocked the sun's rays. The stars around the moon were glistening and glowing red, white, blue, and yellow. I'd never seen the night sky look so brilliant. Amazed by the beauty of this celestial moment, I murmured the Lord's Prayer, and as I finished the last line, "…lead us not into temptation and deliver us from evil, for Thine is the kingdom, the power, and the glory. Amen," a shooting star whisked across the right side of the moon. I stared at the lingering light from it, and then I felt a vibration within my chest. I kept telling myself, *there's something going on here; there's something happening that I can't see.*

At my first opportunity, I went to sleep so I could view that lunar event and understand what that shooting star signified. When I drifted to sleep, I found myself standing in the realm of the Immaculate Absolute and saw Hhere/Ccerdi standing off to my right and smiling at me.

"God!" I said. "I just saw an amazing lunar eclipse, but there's something significant about it. What's going on? What did that shooting star represent?"

Hhere extended his hand, and like an eraser, he wiped away my mental image of the eclipse. I just stared at that particular spot and Touve said, "I want you to see this." Still holding my gaze, I witnessed a beautiful male angel descend gracefully toward earth. His massive white wings had a golden outline. His skin had a faint touch of brown pigment, yet had a white radiance that exuded brightly from out of his pores. While staring at this angel, I realized that he looked familiar, yet the smile on his face suggested that he was not of this world. The angel was descending slowly and picking his spot to sink within the menacing dark cloak that represents the three soul dimensions that vibrate in the Satan Consciousness. This massive angel slowly sunk into this inkwell and made not a ripple. His movement was stealthy, as not to disturb the landscape. Eventually, this angel was submerged completely into the dark matter. I didn't understand what (or whom) I was looking at. Staring at the spot where the angel had disappeared, I heard Touve in the background say to me, "You have just witnessed the arrival of Jesus. December 21, 2010. 1:17 am."

I had awakened around 6:00 a.m., and I didn't have to get back on the road for another five hours. I took this down time to contemplate those words spoken by Touve. He told me that I had witnessed the arrival of the Anointed One, but I still couldn't fully grasp the gravity of such an event. However, what crept into my mind was the question of whether I was worthy of such an event. During the previous months I'd experienced multiple phenomena with aliens and personal conversations with Hhere/Ccerdi. Though speaking and seeing God is most unbelievable and monumental, for some reason, when I was told that I had seen Jesus descend down into our planet, it struck an awkward chord. My mind became overloaded with confusion and conflict about all of these strange occurrences. I had begun to question whether I wanted to pursue this path, and I began to ask myself if I could withstand outside scrutiny if I were to tell others what I had seen.

CHAPTER 17

BEEBE, ARKANSAS

I spent Christmas near Amsterdam, NY, and the landscape of upstate New York didn't hold back with the battering down of heavy ice and snow. Parked at a nearby fuel center, I felt strange to be alone and away from family and friends during the holidays. I'd always made it a point throughout the holidays to be around lots of people. Yet, this time I had to eat a bland Christmas dinner at a truck stop, and it definitely wasn't the same as Grandma's cooking. That Christmas was the first time that I hadn't had the chance to eat my yearly tradition of chitterlings. I don't eat much of them, but I would usually have a small plate of "chitlins" with some hot sauce along with all the other soul food classics, like turkey, ham, fried chicken, stuffing, macaroni and cheese, collards with salt pork, and more! In addition, no soul food holiday meal is complete without my favorite drink to wash that good stuff down: Kool-Aid! Although sad that I didn't have the time to go home, I was appreciative of the meal I had had at the travel center.

On December 29, I was dispatched a load for pickup in Amsterdam, N.Y., and it was to be delivered early January 2, some 1300 miles away outside of Beebe, Ark. It was a late-night load, so I didn't have to pick it up until 9:00 p.m. I eventually picked up the load that evening and began to do all of my paperwork prep. It was around 9:45 p.m. when I started to feel strange. My thoughts were becoming confused about everything I was doing. I kept messing up on my Bill of Laden information, and it felt like my equilibrium was out of balance. I had a hard time

getting my bearing as to where and what I was doing. However strange
I felt, I had to remain focused on getting my trip planning down and
getting on the road. At 10:00 p.m., I departed the shipper and proceeded
to drive through the small town of Amsterdam, N.Y. Navigating toward
Route 5, and then heading toward Highway 30, I had trouble maintaining my focus. Something was seriously wrong, and my wires felt
like they were being crossed. Strangely, I missed my turn to Route 5 and
found myself driving down a road that didn't look truck friendly. There
was only one opportunity to turn the truck around, but once again, my
thoughts felt like they were being jammed. When I missed the moment
to whisk back around, I realized that I was in big trouble. Driving a 74'
tractor trailer with a load of 43,000 pounds, I was driving along what
looked like a residential community. Assessing the situation, I realized
that there was no way I could back up, so my only option was to go
forward and hope that the "trucker gods" were looking out for me and
would give me a nice, wide corner to turn around on and lead me back
to the main road. However, as I crept further up this narrow neighborhood street, the intensity of the trouble began to compound. I came
up to the first corner and negotiated it with no problem. Still, inching
very slowly and at idle speed, I was careful not to hit the many cars that
were parked to both the left and right sides of the road. After turning
right onto this narrow street, I looked ahead and saw something that
didn't look good for me. The corner that I wanted to turn right on had
a car that was parked near the corner on the intersection, closest to my
right, and another one that was parked on the opposite side of the street
and also close to the intersection. In addition, making matters worse,
directly on the right corner was an old wooden utility pole that would
hinder my trailer from turning the corner. I was in a very bad situation.
I approached the corner wide, and made my first attempt to get around
the corner. The first attempt was no good; I tried several more times, but
still couldn't get the nose of the tractor past the car that was blocking the
center intersection, and my trailer was almost scraping the utility pole.
Thirty minutes has passed, and I was stressed out, wondering how to get

that 74' vehicle off that tiny street. I kept jumping out of the truck to make sure I hadn't hit anyone's car or damaged the property. What made me even more nervous was the thought of the residents being awakened by the loud snapping sound of the air brakes being pulled each time I got out the truck. Forty-five minutes had gone by, and I feel helpless as to what to do; I was stuck. I didn't want to call dispatch, as that would have compounded my problems. Realizing that I couldn't get around that corner, I backed the truck up to the center of the street I was on and just sat there in defeat. *What am I going to do?* I asked myself. I was so stressed that it felt like the temperature of the truck was 150 degrees, even though I had the windows down. Controlling my temper and getting quiet so I could think about how to get off that street, I heard the faint sound of metal wind chimes from a nearby house. The melodic sound instantly reminded me of an earlier study of Zen Buddhism and what I learned about being still and naturally following the way. So I sat still and stopped cursing my bad situation. Then my situation opened up for me. The owner of the car that was parked on the opposite side of the street and close to the intersection moved it out of the way. Amazed by the sudden turn of events, I wasted no time taking advantage of that extra space needed to swing my tractor wide to clear the corner. I did it! I got completely around that tight corner and onto a wider road that led back to Route 5. When I got onto that wider road, I stopped and got out and went to check on my trailer to make sure I hadn't damaged anything. When I stood behind the trailer, I felt that same confusing sensation that affected me strangely and caused me to make that wrong turn. I was facing the back of my trailer and looked off to my left and saw a massive and oddly twisted oak tree. Then I became aware of a huge rustling sound above me, and when I looked up, there were hundreds and hundreds of black birds frantically flying about me and racing in and out of that tree. Startled as to what I was seeing, I looked beyond those birds and noticed that the night sky had a strange darkness to it; it looked evil! Keeping calm, I looked within the mass of the birds and that perilous night sky – there was Satan. He was standing within the center of that poisonous scene, and those black birds were wild and loud as they flew within ten feet of my head. I turned the corner of that trailer like I was running the 200 meter dash, jumped in the cab, and speed off while skipping gears! Racing to the safety of Highway 30, my mind became clear, and I regained all of my faculties.

My load plan showed that I had plenty of time to get to Arkansas, even though the trip would normally take about two days. But with new D.O.T. regulations, truckers are to have 10-hour breaks during each day. Therefore, I took my time to get there.

The lull of the road makes everything one big blur, and driving an average of 10,000 miles per month has desensitized my curiosity to see any more farms, rivers, bridges, and road kill. Throughout most of my drive, I was on auto pilot and in a small trance. My thoughts were lucid, and I began to see some spiritual phenomena on the other side. Trying to remain focused on the road, it was difficult for me to see exactly what my third eye was trying to see. However, I sensed a fight. I couldn't determine between whom or what; all I could tell was that there were strikes of lightning thrown back and forth.

A few miles up the road, I pulled into a rest area to sleep. When I stopped the truck, I felt like I was still moving, and my legs felt wobbly. After freshening up, I stepped back up into the truck and jumped in the bunk for rest. Sleep came quickly. Because of my clairvoyance, it didn't take much for me to open up to spiritual phenomena. Also, I'm skilled (internally) to choose what experience I want to come through.

Sleeping agitatedly with a stiff shoulder from driving, I saw something dark and dangerous walking toward me. I recognized his vibration – it was Satan. I immediately flared my white energy bold and wide in a show of confidence and protection. Satan stopped within a few feet of me. To my surprise, I looked off to my right and could see Xzabea staring worriedly at me, as I was standing face to face with the devil! She was viewing us from the ninth dimension and made an attempt to come to my aid, but one of her royal guards held her back as she struggled to get to me. Because of Xzabea's high royal status among her species and chief architect of the hybrid project, she cannot expose herself to any danger outside of her world. To calm her down, I quickly glanced up and gave her a look that said- *I'll be ok!*

The mythological depiction of Satan as red with big scary horns is actually comical. The Satan that stood in front of me was anything but comical. To all those men and women who practice or delve with the black arts or even think they want to worship the Devil: if you were to see the real Satan, the pure fright would evaporate your soul to nothingness! He stood about seven feet tall and had a slender build. Dressed in some strange attire, Satan's garment looked evil, as it was tailored closely to his upper extremities, and as it lowered, the garment flared out near his feet. He wore a spooky-looking brim that was small near the crown, but the rim of his hat was perfectly straight and fierce looking. The hat displayed an important and religious style, with components of a religious relic. I held my ground and didn't cower, and I immediately called from within the power of Jesus Christ to protect me and surround me in his light. While I was positioning myself from strength, I saw Satan's eyes glow venomously green with his hatred of what I was calling forth, and his fists were clenched, as the sound of tightening leather could be heard.

Satan yelled, "Chris Lee!" I didn't flinch and held my ground while his entire presence churned in utter darkness. "You are interfering with matters you do not understand!" he said.

I replied, "I am the son of Hhere/Ccerdi, and I fully serve them and will deliver their message to whoever chooses to listen!"

"Are you aware as to who I am?" The Devil asks.

"Yes, I'm aware of who and what you are," I responded.

"Apparently, you aren't aware of what I am!" says Satan. Then he showed me his mark. The true mark of Satan looked similar to God's mark, yet in between the two sixes facing each other was an upside down mark- an upside down letter T. Admittedly, I was becoming afraid, because his presence was frightening and unsettling. While Satan and I stared at each other, I could see Xzabea from above me pacing frantically.

Dangerously, when I didn't buckle, it looked like Satan was about to lunge toward me. Yet, he paused, realizing that there would be serious consequences if he tampered with me. Therefore, he made a wicked pivot toward his right and looked back at me while dissipating. "You will be watched!" Satan said.

Despite my inner turmoil that night, I surprisingly slept a full 8 hours. Once awake, I was fully aware of my meeting with Satan that night, but I was not perturbed by it. I recorded only what I had seen and heard and commenced my trip toward Arkansas.

On January 2, I had eventually made my delivery outside of Beebe, Ark. There wasn't an immediate dispatched load, so went to a nearby travel center to get something to eat. That weekend the world had brought in the new year of 2011. The roads were quiet, as I assumed that the holiday revelers were sleeping off their liquor. I called one of my friends back in North Carolina to wish her a happy New Year's. After a few minutes of chatter, my friend asked me where I was. I told her that I was in Arkansas. She went on to say that the news informed her that, in the state of Arkansas, people were reporting that black birds were falling out of the sky. She added that people mentioned that it wasn't just a few black birds, but hundreds and hundreds of them falling out of nowhere! Curious, I asked her where the sightings were. Next she told me that the sightings were happening in a town called Beebe. I gasped and told her that Beebe was the town I had just delivered to! *What a coincidence,* I thought. We spoke for a minute or so and hung up. Next, I pulled up the story on the Internet and found that, yes, up to 1,000 black birds had simply fallen out the sky over Beebe. The local authorities suggested that the birds may have suffered shock from the holiday revelers popping loud fire crackers. This is highly plausible, but I couldn't help but replay in my mind the strange events back in Amsterdam, N.Y.; something external was interfering with my thoughts, I had seen hundreds of black birds flying wildly above my head, and I had had a conversation with Satan. This *cannot be a coincidence,* I told myself. *Or could it?* I remembered Satan's last words to me: "You will be watched."

Could it be that, while I traveled to Beebe, Ark., Satan had also followed? Could it be that the lightning strikes I kept seeing in a vision was perhaps God lashing at Satan for tampering with one of his messengers? The notion of it all was very peculiar.

CHAPTER 18

MICHAEL

FEBRUARY 14, 2011 - hour unknown. During a late and cold drive through the state of Ohio, I became very sleepy, and I pulled over to a rest area. One of the annoying things about driving a big rig is trying to find parking late at night. Even at rest areas across the nation, trying to find a parking spot is virtually impossible. It's incredible to see dozens upon dozens of 60,000 pound, 75' foot long monsters parked within 24 inches of each other. Driving cautiously, I couldn't find anywhere to slip in, so I drove to the outside shoulder and shut down for the night.

I'm not sure how long I'd been sleeping, as I eventually found myself standing in the realm of the Immaculate Absolute. This time I saw God in that brilliant synergy form, and while staring at them, I heard Touve instruct me to look up toward the white space as before. I looked up at the same location that Jesus had descended from, and to my amazement, there was another angel approaching. This angel's rate of decent, however, was fast and aggressive. His wings were powerful and extremely large, while his feathers looked dangerous, like swords. This divine angel wore black garb. At first I thought this black attire represented something bad, and then I realized what I was seeing.

"Touve, is this the archangel Michael?!" I asked, excited.

"Yes, I want you to watch this." Touve replied.

Unlike Jesus, who descended to the Earth in a stealthy manner, Michael slammed into the black and filthy conscious realms of man.

When he ripped into it, black matter resembling black paint splashed open from a large hole and exposed the surface level of some location on Earth. I could see down it, and within the exposed area I saw that the archangel had his divinely devout soldiers armed and ready for an epic battle. Instantly, when Michael slammed to the ground like a meteor, he stood courageously, and with a faraway gaze, he looked toward a frightening rumbling from the west.

The anti-Christ was coming and equal to the speed and aggression of Archangel Michael, Satan's approach came within a gigantic, rolling ball of fire. His incendiary rage spit out dirt and ripped through the low conscious levels of its slaves. Ready to meet with a greater force, the arch angel quickly surveyed his forces and then gave a silent command with the flick of his wrist. Before Michael could complete the full motion of his wrist, his entire army shot off like lightening toward Satan and his brood.

Speechless, I realized that a spiritual war was underway, and Archangel Michael had the upper hand. Although this was a dangerous scene to witness, I felt hope that there was someone above who cared for us all on Earth. Even in our most uncertain time and when most of us feel that we've been forgotten, God is constantly protecting and watching over his children. God loves his children; we are all God's children! Because of this great love, he sent one of his most fierce soldiers to begin to save us from the prison and perilous path of Satan.

CHAPTER 19

THE ARRIVAL

FEBRUARY 21, 2011, 11:30 p.m. I had awakened to find myself standing in vast and open plains. Freezing cold, I looked to my right and saw Touve also standing and staring out into this dark landscape. During my travels on the road, this wide countryside looked familiar, yet I couldn't determine the location. Perhaps it was Nebraska or Kansas, even Texas, but I couldn't be sure.

"Touve, I don't have coat on; I'm freezing!" I said.

"Be patient," Touve said, still looking ahead. "You must witness this."

In that grey and heavy hooded robe, a dim and brownish light shone around Touve's mouth with a sinister grin. Watching him, he again instructed me to look straight ahead.

There were no city or town lights on the horizon. A light winter breeze came up from the south, blowing lightly over the tall grass within feet of me. Silence orchestrated the extraordinary event that was about to happen. Like a metronome keeping time, the faint whipping sound of grass being brushed by the winter winds added to the suspense. I stood perfectly still, and then without warning, I heard a large explosion – Boom!

Exploding and being jettisoned from this heartland soil was an enormous and brilliantly white cross that spanned the night sky. Catching me off guard and to my astonishment, I noticed that, on this magnanimous cross was our Lord and Savior Jesus Christ, displayed in the last image in which we remember him. Blasting from deep under the ground was a brilliant and pure energy swirling about Jesus' feet and body, racing to all points on the globe!

This incredible moment took my breath away; I gasped, trying to keep up with the events unfolding. When Jesus blasted from deep within our loam, simultaneously I could see within the lower three dimensions of the Huetpher the people who had become afraid of the arrival of the Messiah. Scurrying like roaches and rats, those non-believers, perpe-trators, and narcissists ran for shelter with visible shame. All of this happened in a split second, and my senses were at high alert. Then I noticed in my right peripheral Touve leaned over and whispered into my right ear, "The Messiah has raised. February 21, 2011, 11:30 p.m."

CHAPTER 20

THE SCRIPT

FEBRUARY 22, 2011, 1:26 am my bizarre experiences over the past year and a half were beginning to take their toll on me. On one hand, my primary focus was to put my life back in order, but on the other hand, I was being forced to open up to contact with other worlds. Not knowing what was going on and why, I felt I'd rather be left alone to enjoy my life. But what was I to do when other beings who have the advantage of being able to travel in and out of our world at will wouldn't take no for an answer? Perhaps this is what people call destiny!

My approach to life is quite conservative, and this diligence is also applied to my gift of other-worldly viewing. Just because I see and hear something that's lofty, dreamy, or euphoric outside of our mundane experience, I will not be quick to receive it. Also, it's a serious struggle and requires lengthy education to understand my visions to the fullest and translate the function of time on the spiritual side and how it measures in our physical space. Therefore, my pragmatism is one of the reasons it has taken me 20 years to reveal my ability. However, this gift of sight keeps me grounded to a certain reality. I mean, who really cares? So what if I can speak, and see, and hear any past historical or famous figure of my choosing, from Mayer Amschel Rothschild to Dr. Martin Luther King? Who would really care that I have such keen sight, that I can look into a person's body and see their ailment, even down to the bacteria strand deep within the tissue of someone's neck. To me, it's just another one of those many unexplainable things under God's sun.

The self-critic is equal to the current conversation I've been having with Hhere/Ccerdi and aliens, yet something deep within me verifies that these experiences are true and aren't to be ignored. Furthermore, my conflicting emotions have become overwhelmed with witnessing the arrival and my conversation with the Jesus.

After speaking with the Messiah, I had become enlivened, yet still perplexed of the tearing effect of two worlds- I couldn't keep silent any longer about it. My opportunity came when Touve called me into his chambers in his realm. Creepily hunched over a device, he was pecking away deliberately. I stood off to his right near the end of the table his was working on. Touve stopped typing and turned his head, staring at me through the dark space within his hood. He silently asked me, *what is wrong with you?*

"Touve, may I speak freely?" I asked somberly. He didn't reply, but held his curious gaze. "I appreciate meeting and having conversations with you. Also, I'm grateful and most privileged to have met God. That experience alone cannot be measured in words. In addition, I'm humbled to have Xzabea come and save me from my own dark hand," I expressed. "Yet, I have to remain realistic about all of this. You must understand, Touve, where I live (America), absolutely no one is going to believe a broke black man! No one will believe me that I've spoken to the one and only Messiah. How are people to take me seriously when I have no title, no peer endorsement, and no power behind me?" I said with disdain. "Besides that, how are people to know that our Lord Savior is here? How are people to realize that the wait is over and that He is here? What is to bring people together in one mind and heart in the name of Jesus Christ?"

Touve didn't respond to me verbally, but pushed a stack of papers down toward the end of the table. The top sheet displayed a line item format, and each line had a typed subject. I looked at the bottom of the page to see a line item that read only a single word: Flood. Puzzled, I looked over to Touve for further explanation. He shifts my focus, and I saw North America at night. Panning east to west, the night lights of our nation's cities were bustling and alive. Then I sensed, among

America's landscape and other land mass of other nations, water beginning to rise up. When I shifted my view further west, I noticed that the state of California was completely dark. Strangely, starting from the top of the state and ending down near San Diego, a single red line was drawn downward. All land mass that was west of this red line fell off into the ocean, causing a massive tsunami wave that slammed into a major section of California. The earthquake and massive flooding was so devastating that the death toll was in the millions; this became the single most devastating event in American history.

"Are you telling me that this natural catastrophe will be the event that'll bring people to Christ?" I asked, stunned. "People are to identify this as the rise of Christ… the Messiah! I don't understand. This cannot be… I have family and friends there!" I cried.

Nothing is spoken between us, so I just stared at this document. I looked at the line items above where it read "Flood" and noticed some recent international events that took place within months of my current dialog. I flipped to the other pages and saw that the following pages line items that were completely filled in had a futuristic tone to them. All of a sudden, I felt something inside me light up!

"Is this a script?" I challenged. "Tell me, what is this… some script or something predestined? Tell me, what I am reading?!" I demanded.

Touve got up from his antiquated black typewriter and walked over to me. He stood about an inch taller than I did, and spoke from the dark of his heavy hood. "Chris, I have known you for a very long time, since December 29, 1969. That evening we first met when you were a child is when you lived with your grandparents on Van Buren Avenue in Peru, Indiana. You don't remember, but we met when you and your grandfather were in one of your favorite hideaways, a little red barn on their property. You were cooking a can of baked beans with meat on an old camping stove. That evening, your grandfather went into the house to get some blankets, and you lay back on an old military cot of his. Sitting atop a dusty workbench was an old radio playing the song, "Theme from a Summer Place," while you gazed beyond the barn doors that were slightly open. An evening star caught your eye, and you wondered whether it was the North Star. What you were looking at was me looking down at you. We both caught each other's eye and made a connection – that was the beginning of our relationship. You were a baby, yet your soul was evolved enough to understand the connection," Touve explained. "Since your first awakening; we'd often meet, and I would teach you the ways of the universe. I didn't expect you to remember any of this as you grew older, and as an adult there would be no way for you to remember anything, because your mind has conformed to the ideas and ways of man. But allow me to refresh your memory and re-explain how God creates," Touve said. "God – Hhere/Ccerdi – created all of the heavens and everything in it; it's perfect. You are perfect! When God creates, they leave nothing to chance, for it's all highly calculated. You've always asked, "What about free will amid a highly calculated world?" and my response is always the same: you've always had and will continue to have the power of free will." Touve pauses. "However, to degrees that none of you can comprehend, you have free will amidst set parameters, set boundaries. Boundaries that lay the framework of something for which all of you suspect that nothing in this world happens by coincidence and this includes chaos and destruction," Touve explained, with calm demeanor. "Where you may see pain and loss, God sees glory and balance without doubt or fear. This is the example that God has been trying to give you. When you're faced with chaos and destruction, don't choose fear and doubt, because God did not invent this; they do not exist. Instead, only choose what arises out of love and promised that all of you are protected in love, happiness, wealth, and freedom. God understands that all of humanity has fallen far from their inner truth, and this is why they have sent their One and Only Son to save all of you for a second and last time. What God asks of all of you is to believe and have faith that their plan is perfect. Also, what God is showing all of you is that the Lord Savior Jesus Christ has risen, and with the power of free will that each of you has been given, you must simply choose and walk in his direction."

CHAPTER 21

No Sympathy for Ignorance

WEEKS had passed since my meeting and conversation with Touve. However, I was still confused and needed some serious contemplation to fully grasp what he had told me about our world and the larger universe having already been designed and written for us. While we're caught up in the tediousness of our small lives, God has already planned and knows the larger direction for humanity; this includes all life in the universe. In addition, Touve explained that God only creates out of love. So my immediate thought was, *If God only creates out of love and if life is highly calculated out of love, then why would they create pain and suffering? Wouldn't this be a paradox?*

Touve was apparently listening to my inner dialog. "Chris, you ask if God creates through paradox. First, you're thinking is too small about this subject. Allow me to illustrate from the position of the Milky Way," explains Touve. "There is no confliction with Hhere/Ccerdi. Their desire to create only expands with clarity. Their first act of clarity was to create the universal plain, and what seems almost unbelievable is that every star, planet, galaxy, nebulae, etc., is exactly where it should be and moves in its inherent vibration; this includes your Milky Way. After God created the physical elements that make up your galaxy, their next act was to go forth unto the many regions and to physically experience it. This meant that God had to manifest in smaller and lower vibrating life forms. But to be able to slow down their state of being, and incarnate and conform to the respective physical elements of any world, God had to first create a supreme physical being that vibrated slightly slower than they, yet one that possessed equal knowledge and secrets of the universe. This divine alchemist contains within himself *every* chemical (organic and inorganic) element, metal, and atomic matter known to both aliens and humans in the galaxy. In addition, this rare being contains within him the "God Spark" that ignites and commands the spirit to life. This supreme physical being is me!" Touve said confidently. "Remember when I told you that life moves of me and spirit sparks of me? Well, I'm the creator of every life form in the Milky Way. Every living creature and every alien and all of you on your planet have some aspect of my Etav. This copper-colored substance contains the intelligence that gives life and forms cellular structure. Also, when I explained to you that your life is part of an unseen structure, though not mechanistic, that unseen structure begins with God forming their clear thoughts about their intentions Thus, this intrepidly begins to follow strict disciplines and calculations of movement. Looking at the Milky Way, God began to wield their intention and brought their idea or Huetpher about Earth to existence. Next, working in tandem with God, I (an extension of them), exercising my free will, created all alien life forms, and the aliens exercising their will and expression brought forth humans. Ultimately, all of this breathing, living, dying, and recreating is a chain of life that allows God to experience it all. It is a perfect order that begins with thought, choice, execution, and experience. There's no misstep or fallacy with God. But none of you on your planet can understand this because of your dark position." Touve paused and momentarily contemplated his next statement. "However, I still have to answer your question: If God's world is perfectly calculated in love, then why create pain? Again, your thinking is too small on this issue. I'm aware of the troubles that exist on your planet, and know that much of the suffering can be eliminated if all of you would stop playing games with yourself. Each of you possesses enough information about yourselves and God to fix your broken world. It's almost laughable when, above you, we see your discontent about silly matters; when in fact, the human race received more divine guidance and information than any other life form in this part of the universe. One of the fundamental problems is that you think that it's all about you. Your narcissism purports that you are the only ones yearning for liberation from pain. If all of you open your eyes and feel from within and know that life outside of you also seeks liberation, each of you would be brought to sorrow to know that there are alien life forms that are born with an imaginable disability to walk. Millions in your world would be shamed for having complained about something petty, such as your body not having enough perfume, when there's an alien race burdened with having to live in odd and heavily elongated bodies that ooze an unsightly thick forming sweat. Now, upon my description about the unimaginable realities some aliens live with, this would suggest that God and I are imperfect. But, I say again, God's way is perfect, even in the awkwardness of an alien being unable to show the expression to weep."

"How is this perfect for the alien who can't show emotion?" I asked, confused.

"Because the aliens who experience something that isn't desirable, or what you call pain, don't see it as any form of torment. For them it just *is*. Rather than complain or make matters worse with worry and fighting, the aliens possessed something within them that allowed them to go beyond their current situation, and this is choice. Alien life understands that the situation they don't like can be transformed into something better or grander. Along the same vein, they also understood that to choose the emotion of pain or to wallow in misery sets a lie in motion. This lie is that they've been alienated, separated from God. Choosing this action suggests that they're not only separated from the greater divine mind, but that they lack the internal knowledge to see other possibilities. However, aliens didn't buy into the lie and chose what is inherently known: that they are born of the divine mind. A divine mind always presents the right solution and direction. Ultimately, the aliens in your Milky Way came together and assessed what could be done to help each other and find a greater path to liberation. This is when humanity was created," Touve explained.

"Obviously, your world has the same power of choice. Unfortunately, your exercising of this powerful action has been misused, manipulated, and misguided. God has sent to your world many teachers to instruct about the ways of inner harmony and true expression. However, rather than learn from these masters and follow your heart and do something grand to achieve liberation, your world chose to remain one-dimensional in your thinking. Therefore, the real question is thus: Do any of you truly want to find liberation, or are you playing games with yourselves?" Touve asked.

"Why do you say that we're playing games with ourselves? I don't think that a woman who's abused by her husband necessarily finds that getting hit in the face is some act of play," I said, irritated.

"Chris, I tell you this. Each and every one of you on your planet is playing games with yourself. Like I said earlier, your world has received an extraordinary amount of information passed down to you about the true way to life and how to expand it. Quite honestly, there's very little compassion left in the universe for a species that is helped over and over again who doesn't respond accordingly. Since the first word was uttered by man, your world has received music, signs, blessings, sages, saints, and miracle upon miracle to remind you of who you are and what each of you are capable of. Yet, you are afraid of yourselves and learn just enough to achieve some instant gratification (usually to cover up some guilt or wrong deed), or most of you mold and twist this powerful information as a law or doctrine to control those who aren't awake – yet." He takes in a deep breath and expands like a cobra. "I add further, choosing the thought of pain not only distanced you from your inner truth, but it also placed your entire world in a false reality that wasn't supposed to exist." Touve paused and looked at me strangely.

"What?" I asked. "What wasn't supposed to exist?"

"When the consciousness of mankind came into his own awareness, thus breaking away from the core co-creators with the hybrid project, he immediately caused himself to forget about his true nature. Autonomy came about, and ignorance set in. As each generation was born, each was born into this retarded (not disability) mindset. You've forgotten about the innate truth and projected pain into every facet of your lives.

This careless action, though unsuspecting, began to form a mind of its own. Pain not only suggests that one is helpless and alone, but more dangerously, it put your world into a position of supplication. This type of action is unnecessary, because it places a person in the position to believe that they aren't capable to helping themselves, and they must rely on someone else. Then this someone, whose heart is filled with malice and ill intent, injects more lies into the person wanting, and manipulation is tooled with fear – the fear that if you don't do this or that, then X will happen to you. The head of this false reality grew and grew, and this designed action took on an identity of its own and fed upon those millions and millions of lives throughout time, lives that chose not to know, listen, and follow their God power within and to liberate themselves from what binds them. Like a flame cooking crack on a dull spoon and evaporating a sickening smell- a dangerous co-dependency was made and mankind poisoned himself. Along with self – torment and unnatural abuse, each of your minds and souls have been corrupted. Consequently, the whole of mankind bowed down and a dark intelligence is validated. Now, all those born unto your world are faced not only with your self-induced curse, but now you also have to live in a world that must choose between God and..." Touve paused again, as if to caution himself.

"Please continue," I said, with suspicion in my voice.

"The dark consciousness that arose from your world dementia automatically created a division on your planet to where now you have to choose between God and something unnatural. In other words, this dark consciousness is Satan. Man invented Satan!" Touve said strongly. "You, your parents, their mothers and fathers, etc., all contributed to it. Every feeling and act of hatred vibrated into a peculiar pattern, and your ill choices would eventually come back to haunt you. But, more than consequential, this peculiar energy pattern contained an intention that was transferred from man's initial self-consciousness – the same awareness that disconnected from the co-creators of the hybrid project. This dangerously low conscious vibration attached itself to your planets' foreign elements, and because of the initial conscious intent, anti-matter was formed. This anti-matter was intelligent and was aware of where it came from – the consciousness of man. Eventually, it began to stir your attention toward the soil and fed your physical impulses. But another problem was perpetuated: the intelligence that transferred from man's consciousness sought autonomy and realized that its expansion and rise was fueled by mankind's desire for identity upon the Earth. With control of itself and involvement in a co-dependent relationship, this anti-matter made its claim upon your planet. This may not be easy to digest, but it was man who invented Satan, as he does not exist anywhere outside your world. Nowhere!" exclaims Touve. "The story about Lucifer being a fallen angel, cast out of the realm of Heaven, is another false reality. I tell you this: Satan (living dark consciousness) was born of an incessant action of ignorance and malaise and was wielded by people and large institutions that benefit from this falsity. However, that is a different dialog." Touve divulges. "Now, your entire world is seriously dysfunctional, and this is the reason that God has created a new plan of action, exercising their power of free will to choose and re-create again and again, until they achieve perfection. Consequently, this is why the new world, Hulligen, exist and the new species, Drixlb, will inherent it. The truth is that Earth and the hybrid project was supposed to be the final stage of the God experience and life harmony within the Milky Way. However, all of you went astray, and that's when God sent his Son to remind you of who you really are. Jesus demonstrated to the world that, even though you are born of flesh, each of you is a powerful spiritual being and is capable of thinking, acting, and breathing beyond the fears of the flesh. However, the whole of you learned nothing, but God is great and loves their children and has sent the Lord and Savior Jesus Christ again to save you. However, this time the divine plan will not be interrupted, because the ill-guided will of man will be no more, thanks to the Drixlb species."

Chapter 22

Dialog with Jesus

ONE day in April, throughout the day, I kept seeing Touve standing between my space reality of the inside of my cab and some invisible realm within the Huetpher. He didn't say anything, just stared at me. This went on for a few hours of him coming in and out of my reality. When I finally got to rest and meditate, I linked to Touve.

"I'm glad you've contacted me. I've shown myself to you throughout your day and would have spoken, but you're not developed strong enough to hear me while awake," Touve said.

"Is there something specific you want?" I asked.

"He wants to meet you!" exclaimed Touve.

"Who?" I asked.

"Jesus."

"What," I said, feeling awkward, "when?"

"Tonight…He will come to you tonight!" Touve stated.

That conversation lasted around five minutes, and I resumed my practice of getting quiet and tried to hold my meditative state. But it was hard, especially since I was fatigued from driving for 11 hours. However, no amount of tiredness would keep me from something as magnanimous as meeting the Messiah. Eventually, I fell asleep. At some point within my deep sleep, I do remember I held the intention to meet Jesus and waited patiently within my inner void. Then I realized that I was gazing deep into space, and I heard a powerfully deep and faraway voice say, "Wait!" The sound of that voice felt like it filled every space within the universe.

But what was even more shocking was that, when this being spoke, I saw an enormous transparent blue face that covered a space wider than the Milky Way. The transparent blue matter was the stuff that the universe is made of. When the face and voice dissipated, I instantly knew why it had urged me to wait. The timing to meet Jesus wasn't right, because I saw in my vision Satan standing behind a tree about 200 feet outside my truck. If the meeting with Jesus would've taken place, we both would have been exposed, and Satan could have slipped into my conscious realm via the Huetpher and caused interference.

Immediately, Touve rushed to me.

"Chris, be careful! Did you see him?" Touve asks.

"At first I didn't, until a light shined from behind him, exposing that he was watching me," I said.

"You must take caution. He knows that he can't harm you, because you're protected. However, he can cause interference in how you receive truth," Touve explained. "Jesus will make a second approach to you. Just be still, and he'll do the rest."

April 21, 2011

I was within days of changing trucking companies my end date coincided with my co-driver's home time, so I drove with him to his hometown of Saltville, Virginia, and from there I departed via Greyhound bus back down to Georgia. But I wasn't to depart until the next morning, so I stayed the might in the truck, parked outside my co-driver's house.

Irritated, I couldn't sleep. Anxiety flowing throughout me, and I felt jittery. My arms and legs felt like electrodes were connected to them and that someone had turned on a slow surge of energy. I got up and shook my hands like I had something sticky on them. In the cab of the truck, the air was stale, so I opened up the curtain and went to let down the windows, until I realized something was watching me in the dark. I calmly sat back on the bunk and watched out toward the tree line about 200 to 300 feet away. Then one of the aliens from the ninth dimension exposed Satan's position with an extremely bright light similar to the blaring lights of a container ship. Satan got out of there in a hurry, and that strange sensation also left my body.

I lay back down, but I still couldn't sleep, and my dry eyes only added irritation to a long and dragging night. Straining, I looked at my phone to see what time it was: 3:00 a.m. Then what I saw next startled me. A huge green light from the northeastern sky shined down on me. Because of my position and liaison with God, Touve, and Xzabea, I understood that Satan would do anything to tear this union apart. Therefore, when that green light came all of a sudden, I didn't know from what source this was coming, so I immediately turned my back to it and tucked myself into a ball. Just in case this was Satan or some other bad intention, it was important that I close off my spiritual ports so that they could not enter.

"It's okay, Chris, that green light is an arrival gift from Jesus to you. He is on his way!" Touve said from a distance.

"Gift" I asked.

"Yes! Use your sight and peer into the green light. Jesus Christ is offering this to you!" Touve instructed.

After only seconds, fascinatingly, I saw the green light beams turn into streams of gold that showered me! Surprised, I said, "More! More!" *Wow, that was awesome*, I thought to myself.

"Now, you must get quiet internally. Be still and create no waves of thought. You must concentrate and be in the moment," Touve instructed.

Touve departed, and I followed his instructions to clear and relax my mind. This was a bit of a challenge, because I had the thought of the green light carrying rays of abundance and shining on me. Yet, I had to be disciplined and ready to face my Lord Jesus Christ.

Poised within the quietude of myself, I only recognize the dark void that surrounded me. Like a beach comber quietly sitting and watching the morning sun rise, I saw a warm glow come out of the void. The glow quickly shined bright and dimmed to an image of a little wooden shack with a tree nearby. The shack was tiny and emitted a strong white light from the cracks of the uneven wood-planked walls. This was no ordinary light; it shone with a brilliance that could only be associated with God. The light that pierced through the wooden door and walls was the white light of Jesus Christ. I stared at it in amazement and took notice of the tree to the right of the shack. The tree looked like an aged oak, yet there was something different about it. The energy that flowed from it suggested that it was not indigenous of Earth's plant kingdom. I could also see that the roots of this tree were virgin, meaning that they hadn't been rooted into the soil long. This tree represented something new. The energy emitted from the shack grew immense, as the light rays from it crossed over into my physical space. My conscious energy meshed with this white energy, and I found myself standing in front of an entrance.

Standing in what looked like a massive foyer, the majestic white and golden walls were quite overwhelming to take in. Before me was an opulent and tall double door. Its long ornamental handles were made of the most pure and finest gold. I stood and stared at the handles; the doors then opened slightly. I took a step back. Opening about two feet, a middle-aged Caucasian male slipped out from behind the door. This divine servant wore apparel that looked exactly like a papal vestment. It was the vestment of ordinary dress, but instead of wearing a zucchetto, which is unique only to the Pope, this keeper of the gate wore a white silk stole with gold-threaded fringes. This loyal man was hurrying me along and opened the doors wider for me to enter. For a moment, I could have sworn that this man was Pope John Paul II. I stared at him in amazement, yet he didn't look me in the face; his attention was on preparing a timely and perfect union between me and Jesus.

Constantly bowing, but not obsequiously, the saint shut the door behind me. Similar to the realm of the Immaculate Absolute, the white space that I stood in was remarkable. Then within 50 feet in front of me, I saw a brownish spot of energy descending toward me. As the brown energy got closer, it started to take form of something that I could recognize as someone with a head, body, and arms. The image became clearer and clearer as it neared me, and then with a quick flash, the Lord and Savior Jesus Christ stood in an elevated position within 30 feet of me.

Next to witnessing Hhere/Ccerdi, seeing Jesus was the most beautiful presence I had laid my eyes on. He had the purest looking olive-colored face, which was crowned with dark brown hair that looked like spun silk. His white robe flowed smartly while in that hovering position, and he had a bright smile that filled me with joy.

"We don't have much time," he said. "Are you ready?"

"I'm not sure what you are asking," I answered. My first thought was that I was about to die. Therefore, I wasn't as quick to answer yes without knowing first what I would be agreeing to.

"The past two years has been a difficult transformation for you. It was a transition that pulled you out of the fray of a world that's full of drifting souls trying to make sense of its existence and to find their piece of happiness. This transformation was forced upon you, and in order for you to have communication with God and Touve, even Xzabea, you had to be reduced to nothing emotionally and materially. Next, we placed you in a position of isolation when you lived in that small town of Hinesville, Ga. We know it was difficult and lonely, but this was the only way for the connection to be had with you. There couldn't be any interference." Jesus said. "I know you have many questions for me, yet this is not the moment to address them. However, there's one question that resonates in the back of your mind, and that is why we picked you," Jesus said.

"Yes, this does consume my thoughts from time to time. The reason I never asked God or Touve why it had been me is because I didn't want to come off as pretentious, and at the same time I didn't want to know, as to not become corrupted with vanity," I exclaimed.

"…and that is the very reason why you were chosen to deliver God's message about 2012. Touve has billions of humans at his disposal; however, what he found in you was a discipline that's unique. We realized that, starting as a teenager, you inherently knew not to convolute your mind with anything that would shape it. It was impressive that, while you learned and lived, you let nothing shape you. You followed a natural vibration that instructed you to remain open. Though not rebellious, you knew that the information about life that was passed down through your parents and whole of society didn't fit or would not serve you. Also, we were happy to see that you had quietly begun a process of mental reduction. It was understood what you were doing. You recognized very early on that you moved with your parents' vibration, and by analyzing your parents and seeing the pain in their lives, you instinctively knew that, just because your parents' lives were a mess, it doesn't mean that you had to follow the same path or inherit their thinking patterns. Consequently, you understood that you had to find the souls' life question of how it wants to express itself and serve others. You knew that, within your parents' life vibration, they had not answered their life question, and subsequently they lived very sad lives and died young. But you avoided the trap of vanity and began your mental reduction to find your life's question. We loved the discipline of dissecting every facet of your personality, condition, idiosyncrasy, fear, lust, sex, hatred, and love. We saw the moment when you discovered you subconscious mind, and that's the moment when Touve decided to use you to speak God's powerful message," Jesus explained.

I stood quietly and internally thanked him for allowing me to be of service. Then Jesus indicated to a point behind me, and I saw a very old tree stump with thick bark rising through the white space. The stump was ancient, and the edge of the stump had a glossed texture from the many hands and feet that had touched or stood on it.

"Chris, you have earned the right to stand on this stump. You've the right to speak God's message about 2012. Don't worry about how it will unfold or who'll choose to listen; this will take a life of its own. Just speak, and speak loudly!" commanded Our Lord. "Yet, before the word of God can be spoken, you have to know the two God principles that all life in the universe abides by: First, do not seek or become dismayed when glory doesn't come your way, even when it's deserved, or if it's stolen from you. Someone will see and know and speak your truth. Second, do not interfere with how others see or find glory, even if you know they are wrong. Contemplation upon a rock can also lead to enlightenment. All evolved life forms in the universe understand and live by these two principles. This eliminates the rise of one's ego and rids of judgment and allows a life, moment, or situation to flow naturally to its own accord, be it positive or negative. It is by these two basic laws that alien societies evolve harmoniously, thus avoiding unnecessary trouble. Also, these laws are the fundamentals to which the Huetpher was built on; it allows free will to take place uninhibited. Your world still has a hard time grasping why some people have a corrupt heart yet are allowed to eat, drink, and live extravagantly while there are people whose hearts are pure like rain and are ignored and left to live in obscurity. Deep within the back of each of your minds, you wonder why God doesn't do anything to correct life's imbalance between the haves and have not. Yet, along the same vein you are quick to reason that it's the free will of each man and woman to choose how to live their life. If their plight is less desirable, they're capable of changing that situation. However, this reasoning really doesn't satisfy your inquiry, but you know nothing else to rely upon, and move on with quiet disdain about life," Jesus explained. "Yet I want each of you to know that these two principles can be unforgiving if not adhered to, especially for anyone knowing these laws. Going against these laws creates unnecessary problems and negative consequences. Once an action has been set forth negatively, these laws will work themselves back to perfection, no matter how long it takes. So, my point in telling you this Is that Hhere/Ccerdi have not forsaken any of you; they see entirely the serious situation that your world is in and have been doing something about it. Slowly and methodically, God has begun planting the seeds in your world that'll change the fabric of your lives. You think God has forgotten the extreme poor while the world's wealthiest stands by and gloats, but you're wrong. You think God allows an evil woman to spew venom upon the life of a good man to go unchecked, but you're wrong. You think that God ignores the private cry of that godly man, whose life has been destroyed unjustly by another corrupt man, but you're wrong. The divine laws of the universe are perfect and self-correcting," Jesus explained. "Just as Touve explained earlier, when struggle arises, each of you feels as if you're alone, but you forget that you are God. Each of you has a God particle within you that contains intelligence and power that's immense. If you only call it in my name and allow this power to overtake your problems, then you'll begin to bring forth happiness and liberation," Jesus expressed. "If each of you would truly practice the art of giving God control, then this would allow your Heavenly Father and Mother to exercise the two universal laws to perfection. By allowing God to express perfectly through you, their will becomes your own will (following what's inherently right) to express and be grand in all that you choose to do and become. Once a person truly understands what it means to let go and allow God to perform their will through them and accentuate this goodness by duplication, then that person is walking along the path of higher knowledge and experience," Jesus said happily. "However, there comes a time when a species can't do any more and its life information becomes dated and no longer inspires growth. Eventually, this species toils and begins to feed on itself and dies. But this is where God takes control and executes a new plan of direction and passes down new information throughout their order of life. This is what all of you are going through now. Your consciousness is growing with new information, and all of you and your progeny are evolving into the new life as a Drixlb species. The Drixlb species is the answer, as it will alleviate humankind's never-ending drama. When all of mankind completely transforms into this most evolved species, you will never want to go back to that lower vibration known as humankind," Jesus said, joyfully. "However, we know that, beyond these words, tomorrow you'll slip back into worry and hopelessly rely on the same books, talk, preach, and lament in search for solace and inspiration. You'll still cement your inequities about the world with hatred, and the less fortunate will continue to weep. Sadly, your lives continue to swing between hope and despair. We know that it's challenging for all of you to keep your faith in God when all around you seems lost. We're also aware that the words and deeds of your power elite, wearers of religious cloth, and public figures has caused most of you to lose faith in humanity altogether. Again, you're limited to the resources and information that'll transcend these worn-out conditions and circumstances. So to echo a question you asked Hhere/Ccerdi, "What else are you to do? How can we be more than the information afforded to us?" The answer to those questions has unfolded through you, Chris," Jesus exclaimed.

The New Tree of Knowledge: Yevela

"All of this knowledge that has been passed down to you, such as God's true name, the true origin of humanity, the rise of the Drixlb, and the identity of Touve are secrets contained within then new tree of knowledge from the planet Hulligen, called Yevela – The Tree of Christ Knowledge. Now, these secrets have been revealed to you, because in your deep soul searching, you triggered a beautiful phenomenon to begin unraveling. Ultimately, one miracle led to another, which led to God, and by consciously connecting to them, you ate the fruit of the Yevela Tree of Christ Knowledge. The fruit of the Yevela tree represents transparency and revelation," Jesus said.

"What does the Yevela fruit look like?" I asked.

"The fruit of this tree is the most coveted within the Milky Way. Like the size of a kiwi fruit, the Yevela fruit is clear and amber in color, and its texture is like hardened jelly. Even the thin skin of this fruit is transparent, for you can see the six seeds in the middle of the fruit. Every Yevela fruit has exactly six edible seeds. When you consume this fruit, its seeds' sparks instantaneous conscious uplift. An elusive spiritual block is aligned and removed; ultimately, the conscious rise becomes permanent and can never be reversed. Growth is inevitable. The Yevela tree of knowledge is offered to all on your planet, and the connection to this eternal truth will be through me. I am the gateway between man and God," said Jesus. "Each of your soul yearns to grow. It wants this great spiritual awakening to happen so it can expand to have greater experiences and freedom. Coded within your souls is the command to search for the Yevela tree. Over thousands of years and countless lives, a soul keeps rising and presents a question to its host: What is my life question? The soul will not stop until it finds its truth in the grand scheme of things. It seeks to be rid of its dark matter (dogma, lies, negativity), and rise to a higher truth," Jesus said. "Through me, each of you shall eat the grandest fruit in the universe, and your life will never be the same. Your petty ways in life will embarrass you; it will be revealed that all of you have wasted precious time. In addition, by eating of the Yevela tree, a person makes huge and lasting changes in their lives to reflect their conscious shift. Like I said earlier, once a person connects with the Yevela Tree of Christ Knowledge and eats its fruit, the conscious uplift is permanent and cannot be reversed. So whoever makes this connection cannot go back to their ignorant ways or turn a blind eye to the wrongs of your life. The rise in conscious is a serious event, and once a person's soul finds this truth, it will kick, scream, and fight to do right in life. Ergo, it would not be wise to go against the grain of this rare and tremendous spiritual connection," Jesus explains.

CHAPTER 23

AFTER OBAMA

LISTENING intently, my conversation with Jesus lasted for over two hours. However, in the back of my mind, a previous conversation with Touve repeated itself. I was disturbed by the foretelling of the tragedy that would hit the entire state of California, especially when I have loved ones living there. One of my challenges with and concerns about this information was getting Touve to tell me when this would take place. Touve did not give me the date of this catastrophe; however, it's a matter of me being able to translate this doomsday period from this outer world to our physical space. Time outside of our reality doesn't conform to anything we design to measure. Touve had shown me on that day of February 22 the number 58. I thought he was telling me that 58 days from Feb 22, California would suffer this huge crisis. But I was wrong, not realizing he was addressing two different subjects in the same vision. The 58th day from February 22 was April 21, and it was that day I changed companies and the same morning when I saw that green light shine on me from above (Jesus' welcoming gift).

Therefore, getting the date of disaster was especially challenging for me. Concentration is key, but concentration is hard to keep with the constant rumbling of a truck engine. I have to be accurate here, as the whole purpose of this information is not only to be revealing, but also to serve as a warning to those who live in that western hemisphere.

When Jesus finished speaking, I felt Touve's conscious mesh with mine, thus changing my focus from the Messiah to his. Now, any opportunity to connect with Touve is not only important, but fleeting. He's an extreme recluse and is impatient; if your thoughts are not clear, then he'll dismiss you as fast as you can scratch.

Making sure I was centered, I asked Touve, "I'm having a difficult time understanding the timeline of the catastrophic flood that will hit California. Will you help me understand this?"

"Slow down your thoughts, and focus intensely on what I'm going to show you." Touve instructed.

The Vision

President Barack Obama was speaking at the time that he was elected. The mass conscious energy around him was fairly positive and upbeat and somewhat dim in coloration. As the mass conscious energy moved forward like a wave, President Obama was standing before it with his mouth open. His breath matched the flow and positive vibration of the wave of energy. However, as Obama continued to speak, both his breath and the mass energy behind him turned black. It was as if the president was blowing out pure black smoke. Next, I saw a massive slate of rock with the number 212 stamped on it and an elongated fissure that was beginning to shift, causing opposite sides of the slate to separate.

Understanding the Vision

First, this vision was not telling me that the president was of dark energy, but that he represents a certain upcoming period in American history. The natural catastrophe that'll hit this nation will be a major blow to our commerce and our complete way of life; in addition, it will test our spiritual resolve. This shocking event will also grip the attention of the international community. Next, the number 212 reference was a difficult one to interpret, because I wasn't sure if Touve was saying 212 days or whether he meant February 12. However, I felt it was 212 days. Translating time from the realms beyond our physical reality is extremely hard to do; at least it is for me. But, upon serious contemplation, I'm quite sure it's 212 days. Ergo, having asked this question on June 4, 2011, the 212nd day from the date of inquiry is January 2, 2012. In other words, Touve was telling me that the catastrophic flood will hit on that date or that this date marks a shift below California's surface and will develop into a massive earthquake and flooding by the seventh of that month. It will be the single-most shocking and crippling moment in American history since the attack on Pearl Harbor.

I still had a hard time processing what had been shown to me, because for me, this was personal. My brother and sister live in Santa Monica, so the thought of them becoming victims of what's to come is very disturbing. Since my emotions are mixed and might interfere with my time translation, I was reluctant to release the information included in this book. However, Touve had become irritated at my vacillations and adamantly instructed me to record the vision and not to worry about time. While contemplating, I saw Touve step out from my consciousness and walk into the realm of the Immaculate Absolute. He was standing in front of that vertical band of energy (the strand of human consciousness and souls), that Hhere was monitoring at some point in our past conversation. He turned the energy band on its side and took his index finger and measured up to three inches of a specific section of it. The section of consciousness energy he was focusing on had an eggshell coloration to it and like slicing through salami; Touve slipped a thin black board between the sliced area.

"What is that?" I asked Touve.

"This black board is live dark energy and contains information that will put the entire human consciousness into mass reflection and malaise. This forced spiritual dark moment must first begin with America, because your nation was the first geographical platform that involved multiple races of people starting to mix and intermarry within the Hybrid project. America was and still is the ground for life evolving itself, however difficult it may be. This calculated sequence will be far reaching to international waters and will strike fear into every human being on this planet. Every man and woman will be forced to reflect upon their lives and each other. In each of you there will be deep pain, as you toil and reason regarding what has just hit your nation, but your logic will not satisfy you. Your cut will be so deep that, no matter how much you'll try to cover it up and go about business as usual, the unease will keep tapping away at your psyche and pit your false ego and your suppressed inner truth against each other. Still fighting to keep your existing way of life, this catastrophic event will overshadow your pettiness and senseless ways and wash your hearts in loneliness and uncertainty," Touve explained.

August 23, 2011, 11:29 p.m., Martinsburg, WV

I had made plans to prepare this manuscript for editing, but there was much frustration in my search for an editor. Therefore, each day that I didn't get this work reviewed only pushed my plans to deliver this message back a bit further. At this hour, I'm sitting in the cab of my truck, tired after a long drive from Oklahoma City, Oklahoma to Martinsburg, W.V. I drifted off to sleep and within an instant, I had three visitors: Jesus, Touve, and Stern (one of the principle Layonians). Their sudden presence told me that there's some serious business to be had. Jesus and Touve didn't speak, as Stern was the communicator this evening. However, the presence of our Lord and the universe's chief alchemist and engineer reassured me that the receiving message from the Layonians was safe and true.

"How may I help you, Stern?" I asked.

"Your nation's capital just had an earthquake on August 23; is this correct?" asked Stern.

"Yes, this is what I've heard, but I've been driving for the past two days, so I don't know the details," I explained.

Stern waved his hand for me to connect to his realm. "I want you to find the closest tree and connect to the ninth dimension.

As soon as I made connection, I sat in one of their control rooms within a Super Science Complex. I sat calmly, and then Stern streamed a stunning vision.

In a barren desert, a dead white dove sank eerily into the sand. Next,

I saw our nation's capital, yet while looking at this powerful image, the ether or space around the capital and other structures shifted strangely. It shifted awkwardly to the left, yet there was something sinister within the pivot of the shift. Something was taken, but what?

Monitoring my vision, Stern guided me through this live maze. "Okay, I want you to look here. Remember that earthquake. Look again."

I shifted my focus within the vision. Transitioning from the public information about an earthquake that hit the D.C. area, I saw a gigantic underground tunnel. I was standing on the completed side of this tunnel that featured new concrete walls and road. Stern showed to me that I could fit my 75' long and 13'6" tall semi-truck through it. Looking around, I realized that before me was a recent and blasted opening to somewhere else. Near this dark opening was fresh concrete rubble strewn about, and white rock dust still hovered over my head. Curious, I asked Stern to reveal what was beyond the dark side of this tunnel.

"Look right here and you'll see that this tunnel extension leads to an enormous underground facility," Stern said, while guiding my thoughts slowly.

When Stern moved my thoughts slowly to the right, I saw a massive underground building, yet it looked more like a hangar. Engineers and workers and staff members worked in secrecy, unaware that I was suspended above them- watching. Then, to confirm my suspicions that this was some underground hanger, I saw a tail end of a huge passenger jet. Maintaining concentration, I began to wonder why something like this was built. Then Stern shifted my focus again, and I saw dignitaries and powerful figures in D.C. with their families, hurrying down huge concrete stairs that led underground. I was stunned to realize what was being suggested by this vision. There was something sinister about it, because whatever the reason for this deep underground facility that is heavily fortified with concrete and iron apparently reserved for the privileged, the reason can't be good.

"Stern, where is this facility?" I asked.

"There are many extensions, but the main part is deep within Pennsylvania," Stern said. "Keep watching."

I lost concentration within my vision. But then I traced this information energy strand from the beginning and kept following it to a new connection. In the back of my mind, I searched for the reason for building this bunker and wondered why only people who seem to have privilege would be saved. Next, in answer to my self-inquiry, I saw a black nuclear warhead with the markings of "U.S.A." on the side. After seeing this warhead, I saw the image of the Star of David. Immediately after that, I saw the nuke missile rise out of its silo.

I was frightened. "Stern, wait!" *My god, what am I getting myself into?* I thought. "Is the course of this missile going toward Israel or launched out of Israel?"

"It is being launched out of and toward further East," Stern said, calmly.

I immediately disconnected myself from this ominous vision and stepped outside for air. Yet within five minutes, I felt a vibration from Touve wanting me to re-connect with him. Jumping back into my truck, I lay down on the bunk and immediately went into meditation.

"Chris, this truth had to be revealed to you, but this vision and information are also an extension of an earlier dialog we had about the Obama presidency. If you remember that dark energy board you saw me place into the mass consciousness of humanity, that tightly constructed energy mass contains a lot of information. As I explained, there are codes within that live and intelligent module that'll set your world on a different course, and yes, this course will be sorrowful and distant. However, there's irony within this dark period, as it will help your world to avert an irreversible disaster. Your world is teetering on a precipice of something none of you want to be a part of. Your world peace has vanished, and Satan's control will be cemented if the controllers of western and eastern nations don't pull back from tyranny and greed. Their deep ignorance and lack of humility are literally about to split your physical world in half," Touve explained. "But we are not going to let this happen. In response to every powerful culprit that ravaged this planet and each one who hoarded abundant elements and materials given of your planet and withheld from the starving and needy, we will reverse their plans. Just as I explained before, Hhere/Ccerdi is perfect, and likewise is their movement. Ergo, the plan of the darkened heart is no match for them, and it is unnatural and only temporary. Ultimately, when your entire world is in chaos and none will know what to do, there will be instruction for each of you to get quiet." Touve looked at me with a smile. "Get quiet, and a realization will come upon each of you. Beyond the damaged part of your soul lies quietly a purity that awaits the divine connection. When all of you are suspended into an abyss of anguish, that very tiny speck of good within your heart will illuminate toward the heavens, and that's when the Lord and Savior Jesus Christ will reach in and pull you back into the light," Touve said. "After this dark phase, your world will not be the same. There will be a tremendous rise of consciousness, a better willingness to live amongst each other. Furthermore, the union between man and alien will form. This higher intelligence will help, heal, and expand your world."

CHAPTER 24

THE PERFECT EXAMPLE

ONE evening in July, I couldn't sleep, due to stress from being tugged and thrown around by that truck. Although I had the power to meditate when I'd become emotionally overwhelmed, the thought of concentrating just to quiet my mind sounded daunting, as It takes much energy to quiet the mind. However, I had to do something, because the mental strain was particularly high that day, and it felt like my head was going to explode. Focusing on my breathing, my thoughts began to slow down, and I had begun to feel sedated. How long I was meditating was unclear, yet as I went deeper into the abyss of my center- a slow and rolling white fog appeared. During meditation, it is important not to become distracted by internal elements that'll rise and fade, so when that fog was revealed, I knew not to attach any thought to it. Silence dominated my inner experience, but my passive awareness stayed focused on that fog. For some reason it lingered for a while, and then my distant curiosity took on a bit more interest. I began to move toward the fog; yet, a strange inclination came over me to move very slowly and quietly. The closer I got, the quieter my surroundings became. The air of silence was beyond anything that I could describe, and it felt like there wasn't any macro- or micro-electrical disturbance in any degree. When I got even closer to the wall of the fog, I noticed my approach from the right was at a strange angle similar to a marine drill marching the oblique. Moving extremely slow at a 45 degree angle and closest to the left edge of this white fog, I felt that the space around me was more than pure. It was a feeling similar to the realm of the Immaculate Absolute. I approached the left end of the fog and stopped. From the other side, a brilliant light shined outward past me, and then it dimmed a bit. I held my position, reluctant to look around the corner of this fog. Like a little boy peeking around a cement wall to peek at the older kids playing after his momma told him he's too young to play, I couldn't resist the temptation to look. Something in the back of my mind cautioned me to slow down, but If I were to look that I'd better be quieter than I've ever in my life. The divine light shining from around the corner was beckoning me. I moved very slowly and deliberately, careful even to control my breathing. Each movement brought me closer to seeing around the corner, and as I revealed my face, rays of beautiful warm light touched my skin. Looking beyond the warm light, I saw something extremely precious and awe inspiring. I stood with half of my face around the corner of the fog and noticed that I was positioned behind some brilliant yellowish-white object. When the brilliance dimmed a little, I realized that the object was Jesus Christ kneeling and bowing. His form and peacefulness filled me with emotion, but I dared not flinch so as to not disturb this rare moment. I controlled myself and looked to see before whom Jesus was kneeling. Beyond the scene was the massive universe. Voluminous with stars and galaxies and new worlds, the universe was filled with an enormous and powerful intelligence. I remained partly behind the fog to remain hidden. While amazed to seeing Jesus praying beautifully, I saw a flash from a deep part of space as though the universe was winking at me and saying, *we see you!* My heart started to beat a bit faster when a light breeze embraced my face, yet there was something familiar about the feel of that breeze. Then it hit me; I had just felt Hhere/Ccerdi. Subtlety, they were saying that they wanted me to witness this moment. As Jesus remained kneeling and bowing, I heard God say to their Son, "You are the perfect example, and all under our eyes shall live your example."